MW01094211

CONFEDERATE
ORIGINS OF
UNION VICTORY

CULTURE AND DECISIONS IN WAR

Confederate Origins of Union Victory

Culture and Decisions in War
An Argument

Steven Hardesty

Stevens & Marlin Publishing, LLC
Sarasota, Florida

Copyright © 2016 by Steven Hardesty.

All rights reserved. No part of this publication may be reproduced, distributed or transmitted in any form or by any means, including photocopying, recording, or other electronic or mechanical methods, without the prior written permission of the author, except in the case of brief quotations embodied in critical reviews and certain other noncommercial uses permitted by copyright law. For permission requests, write to the author at the address below.

Steven Hardesty
Stevens & Marlin Publishing, LLC
PO Box 4006
Sarasota, Florida, 34230 USA

www.stevenhardesty.com
www.stevensandmarlinbooks.com

Cover Design by Megan Crewe at www.megancrewe.com
Cover Image by Depositphotos
Book Layout © 2013 BookDesignTemplates.com

Confederate Origins of Union Victory/Steven Hardesty —1st ed.
ISBN-13: 978-1-9833-2897-8
20161004/20180701

Four things greater than all things are,
Women and Horses and Power and War.

– Kipling

CONTENTS

Introducing the Argument

THE LOST CAUSE WAS NOT LOST by the South, it was thrown away in a story gaudy and bizarre – of a Confederate general in 1864 who fought a dogged delaying action before a huge Union army led by a commander now legendary for his relentless drive, buying for the Confederacy the precious time that might secure Southern independence, and how that general, for his achievement, was thrown aside for a hot-blooded young man so determined to attack his enemies that he destroyed his own army. In the course of these disastrous events, the South's second greatest city – Atlanta – fell to Northern power, the Confederacy's bread basket was scorched in Sherman's March to the Sea, and the last large Confederate force still able to maneuver in the field – the Army of Tennessee – was smashed, ending the dream of Southern nationhood. What made it all happen?

People go to war for many reasons but culture decides *how* they will make war. The South allowed victory in its 1861-65 rebellion against the United States for independence and to preserve slavery to bleed away because its military and political leaders could not recognize and transcend the limits of the culture that made them. That is the argument of this book.

In the war's most critical year, 1864, the South's hyper-aggressive, inflexible, and parochial leaders, encouraged by their people, chose a hot-blooded young commander, General John Bell Hood, to drive the Confederate States Army of Tennessee from Georgia toward the Ohio Valley to cut in two the rump United States and liberate the South. The choice of man and strategy made sense in the context of mid-nineteenth century Southern culture. But the man and the campaign he made cost the South its last chance for success.

The disaster Hood created in his Middle Tennessee Campaign, and the fantasy that drove him to it, illustrates the Confederate origins of Union victory in the U.S. Civil War. But the answer to *why* it happened lies deep in the cultural attitudes of the South at the middle of the nineteenth century with an economy and white society supported by a working class of black slaves. Why this man Hood, who was not the Civil War's best or worst general but a man crippled in love, body, and spirit, came to be in 1864 the only general who could win the war for the South and why the South would not let him win the war it had so fervently wanted is the story of how the Lost Cause was thrown away.

While the argument here focuses on the South, a similar story can be told of the North at mid-century. The North's obstinate adherence to its own cultural limits in choosing strategy and leaders had the Union floundering in failure for three bloody years until the surprise upshot of General Ulysses S. Grant with a radical new concept of modern warfare. Until Grant, the North was no more immune to its own unexamined cultural debilities than the South.

Understanding the cultural factors that drove Southerners to their choices in Confederate military strategy and commanders is to understand why any country goes to war, how it fights, and why it wins or loses. Why did the Confederacy allow its choices to become so limited that John Bell Hood was all the South had to place at the balance point of victory and disaster in the Civil War's last year, and could we Americans do that to ourselves again?

Part I

Making the Confederate War

THERE ON THE HORIZON, across the rolling Georgia plains sunk in midnight gloom and the still unsettled dust of summer's last day, the city of Atlanta flashed, flashed, and flashed again, throwing up gouts of orange and red. Union cavalrymen and horses pounding south, artillerymen hauling their guns west, and infantryman shoving north all turned their faces toward the city at the first shattering roar of the explosion. It ran through the ground and shook the earth beneath the soldiers' shoes. It was like the beginning or the ending of a world.

Their red-bearded commander in Union blue, far south of the city and sitting on a tree stump writing new combat orders, turned startled. When he heard the pulsing follow-on explosions, he thought the artillery of his own army was moving in to take the city. The men around him cheered.

Then they shouted for the chance to bag the enemy army as well on this last morning of summer in the war's fourth year, 1864. *Let's go smash them, Uncle Billy! Smash them, win the war, and go home!*

Across to the west, the young commander in Confederate gray, one-armed and one-legged and strapped onto his saddle, an aide carrying his extra cork leg made in France, had his bands strike up "Lorena," a tune of loss and yearning, and led the main body of his army away from the city and the closing pincers of his red-bearded enemy. Behind him, his army's ammunition and supply trains, eighty-one carloads, continued exploding in Atlanta's rail yards, blowing away a battle's-worth of powder, shot, and shell. Bombs corkscrewed through the smoke and bullets hissed down the streets. The half-burnt city began to burn again.

Nearly by the force of his anxious will alone, the young general dragged his 40,000 men away from the burning city and the closing grasp of his enemy, hauling with them tons of metal in guns and shells, spare horseshoes and smithy's anvils, tons more of fabric in tents and flags, wagonloads of food, leather, grease, fodder, medicine, and all the other needs of an army on the march to a new fight.

This was an army that had grown accustomed to nonstop combat and to the bitter disappointment of error and failure. It had lost six battles in six weeks and now it had lost its city-base and trainload of munitions. An enemy rich in battalions and in every tool of war was coming after it, led by a red-bearded commander frightening for his refusal to be beaten away from what he wanted.

And this gray army was an army with a mutinous reputation for throwing off failed commanders. The young man strapped in his saddle had to think of that, as he had to think of the rebel president who had put him here to defy his political enemies, of the newspapers that had bawled for him to drench them in Yankee blood, of a Southern population that cheered him as chief among a younger generation of war-winners, of his own back-stabbing greed for command, and of how all this was wrapped up in a girl in Richmond, Virginia, who might or might not be his. He had given her his diamond-studded general's star as a marker of his love but what did it mean to her? This golden warrior and battered general, dreaming himself the liberator of his nation, was Confederate General John Bell Hood. Now he had to think of his war gone sour and with it all his dreams.

But there was battle-fire in his eye still and his Confederate States Army of Tennessee was made up of long-legged, long-striding Westerners who had whipped and been whipped and come back to fight again. They were men of grit who made up a huge and flexible military power that, guided by a good new counter strategy, could shatter this vast Union invasion. Hood had the strategy. He had the army. And he was Hood. Out of those things he expected to fashion a victory to redeem himself in Georgia.

Then he would appall the enemy with a counter invasion that would free his own great commander, Robert E. Lee, from entrapment in Union General Ulysses S. Grant's tightening siege of the Confederate capital at Richmond. Their two armies combined, Lee and Hood, mentor and pupil, would sweep on to Washington City to raise their red battle flags over the enemy capital, end the war, and free a new nation, the Confederate States of America. After that, what would come next for Hood but glory, his chosen girl, and a boundless horizon?

But first he had to whip red-bearded Major General William T. Sherman and 120,000 Union men in blue.

Yes, it could be done. Lee, in repeatedly beating the United States Army of the Potomac in numerically mismatched fights, proved that victory in battle is not always about troop numbers. More often, it is about a commander's plan of attack filled with surprise and fury combined with each soldier's rabid determination to kill and win. Hood and his troops had those qualities but what they lacked was more fundamental. They were not supported by a Confederacy prepared to win its war. The reasons are few and stark and rooted in the cultural attitudes of the South in the middle of the nineteenth century.

Five critical cultural attitudes help explain Confederate failure and make the argument of this book. These attitudes were shared to some degree by all Americans in the North and West as well as the South at the time. But their more intense expression in the South undercut the Confederate war effort:

> *First, prideful hot blood.* The Southern self-image of hot-blooded and uncalculating actors made most people and leaders of the Confederacy unable to accept and exploit a potentially war-winning, purely defensive military strategy proposed by their president, Jefferson Davis. Southerners had to have action. A long, slow defense to wear down Northern morale and Northern armies failed the Southern craving for rapid action no matter the cost to a resource-poor Confederacy.

> *Second, determined insularity.* Southerners' lack of understanding of and disinterest in the larger world outside the South, compounded by a lower rate of literacy, prevented the South from using cotton to draw in other nations to create a world war for Southern liberation. Many in elite classes in Great Britain and France yearned to help the Southern insurrection in order to break up the United States to end its growing economic and political threat to European ambitions.[1] But Southern leaders' insularity resulted in failure to understand how to use that hunger to internationalize their war.

> *Third, defensive inflexibility.* Southern leaders considered they must appear inflexible in favor of the South on every political, economic, social, religious,

and national expansion issue because they had to be inflexible on the issue of black slavery. They considered slavery under increasing attack. Showing weakness anywhere imperiled the slave system as protected by the U.S. Constitution and a Federal government dominated by Southern power. To risk the slave-based economy risked destruction of the entire Southern social system.

Fourth, inflexibility in strategic planning. Strategy is the method of relating means to ends under the stress of events to achieve an objective. That makes strategy a shape-changeable creature as the interplay of the combatants' competing intellectual and physical powers act upon it. Strategy-makers must be broadly versatile, continuously evaluating their strategic concepts and plans as they seek to anticipate an enemy's intent and counter his moves. The South's defensive inflexibility in defense of slavery produced inflexibility in war-fighting strategy.

Fifth, self-defeating racism. In a slave population of four million in 1864, there were enough black men to replenish combat casualties and desertions in the rapidly depleting Confederate armies and to make up whole new armies. But, as Confederate Vice President Alexander Stephens said, "With us all the white race, however high or low, rich or poor, is equal in the eyes of the law. Not so with the Negro. Subordination is his place. He by Nature, or by the curse against Cain, is fitted for that condition which he occupies in our system."[2] Arming black men to fight for white freedom would invalidate the entire rationale for the Confederate war and could not be allowed.

These five chief aspects of mid-century culture combined to make inflexible the Confederacy's administration of the Southern war. They denied the South the ability to evolve military strategy and choose combat commanders capable of supporting a national strategic plan that more effectively used the South's limited human and material resources. That, in turn, denied the South the tools to beat off the commanders and strategy which the North, after three years of its own error and failure, finally developed to win the war to preserve the Union.

All this was multiplied by one more curious factor – a long-developing cultural civil war within the South made by whites rebelling against a perceived African-ness inflicted on them by their own slaves.

* * *

MEETING THE SOUTH AT MID-CENTURY

The South was populated largely by the cattle-, hog-, and sheep-herding people of Scotland, Wales, and Ireland. In America, they became people-herding people. Much of the Deep South was like tropical Africa – a misery of heat and humidity, a land quickly overgrown, full of things that bite and sting, with waist-high ant towers, tornadoes, hurricanes, and malaria. White people so filled these tropics with slaves kidnapped or bought out of Africa that some southern states – Mississippi and South Carolina – became majority black in population and Alabama, Florida, Georgia, and Louisiana nearly so. In this environment, and over the two centuries before the Civil War, white and black sucked at the same black teat in the nursery, spoke the same "Mammy English," reinforced each other's folk cultures, and augmented the power of slavery by a master-and-man interdependence. While the North shook off slavery as an immoral economic tool, the South considered black slavery and the white society that sprang from it as fixed and unchangeable.

Of the United States' 31 million people in 1860, four million – thirteen percent – were enslaved blacks and one-half million were free blacks. Another 340,000 were Native Americans/Indians. Most enslaved blacks and half of free blacks lived in the eleven southern states that rebelled to form the Confederate States of America.

White society North and South in the first half of the nineteenth century was raw. Slavery was enforced by lynch law and national statute, by the tearing apart of the slave family, and by white and black illiteracy. Whites made war on Indians to clear them away as impediments to national expansion. Governments and the courts were loose, disorganized, and corrupt. "Justice" issued from community prejudice or was bought by corporate powers, such as the cotton industry and the railroads. Women and children had few legal rights and little defense against abuse. The country was an alcoholic republic of brutal corporal punishment, child labor, the chaining of lunatics, and the overwork and abuse of animals.

In governing himself and the United States, the pre-war, adult white male American showed little enthusiasm for the rights of others except as they reinforced his own. But he demanded absolute respect for his own rights and for the freedom to define those rights as he saw fit, and to compel others, particularly the government, to acknowledge and provide for those rights.

Americans then, as now, claimed to despise powerful central government with its taxes and conscriptions. Yet Americans demanded tremendous services from that government – highways and waterways, railroads, clearing Indians from the West, subsidized frontier land.

In its long political control of the national government – from adoption of the U.S. Constitution in 1789 to secession in 1860 – the South channeled government benefits toward itself, in good American political fashion, and built legal protections for slavery. Among these was the draft Thirteenth

Amendment to the U.S. Constitution proposed in 1861 and intended to prevent the Federal government from interfering in state laws protecting slavery.[3] The South revolted into secession only when its control of the national government was threatened by demographic and economic changes reshaping American politics and by a freak of a political party – Abraham Lincoln's "Black" Republicans – that hated slavery more than it loved traditional party self-aggrandizement.

With or without a Republican Party determined to abolish slavery, revolutionary change was coming into the United States, change swift, exciting, frightening, and exhausting. The great cities of the North were rebuilt so rapidly, and rebuilt again and again, that a man and woman at middle age could not recognize the neighborhoods of childhood. The old New York, said Edith Wharton, in words grand and sad, was Atlantis, lost and never to be found again. That was true of much of the urbanizing North. This whirlwind of change brought a great step up in the comfort and sanitation of everyday living. New-built city houses were equipped with cast-iron cook stoves that produced piped hot water, with iceboxes, steam heat, toilets, and bathrooms attached to city sewers, and, in a few precincts in a few Northern cities, piped, potable drinking water.

Fewer of these changes easing the burdensome chores of everyday life were adopted in the South. Most Southerners saw little need for them as their ample slave labor force already performed all those tasks for white society. Poor white

Southerners on their scattered farms could not afford these innovations any more than they could afford slaves.

Alongside and in part brought on by these physical innovations came a shift in the way Americans thought about themselves and their nation, bringing into public discussion new ideas the South felt compelled to resist. Technological change and the idea of love, or the popular concept of romantic love invented in the eighteenth century and made maudlin in the nineteenth, combined with the religious revivalism of the early 1800s to shove Americans toward a new attitude toward others. Romance brought Americans to a new empathy for the halt and the lame, the insane, animals, and those enslaved. This logic of romance blended with religious revival – the Second Great Awakening in the first half of the century – to open American minds to a broader reading of Love Thy Neighbor. Few Americans considered or wanted to consider the frightful end to which this new logic could lead. But these new attitudes, confused and confusing, seemed to many people to call for less selfishness in personal and public life and more generosity of spirit.

In that peculiarly American way of driving all things to their extreme, some people began to demand of themselves a larger vision of their lives and that meant they must demand a larger vision for the national life. The future – all those cast-iron cook stoves pumping out hot water to bathe fat babies, all those factories churning out life-easing goods – no longer had to be a string of lifetimes down on the farm, one dull-witted, barefoot generation after another, each child's life little different from that of its parent.

No, now there could be something more, something grander for each American, something that required individual responsibility and self-sacrifice in down payment. When Northern men and women, and some in the South, became infected with this idea and looked at slavery, they were surprised to find a personal call to duty. The call to abolish slavery. They felt compelled to accept the responsibility to make a change in the nation's way of life, as terrible and frightening as that change might become.

* * *

American slavery is a curiosity among world slave systems because it was based entirely on race as demarcation between master and man. But it began with a more traditional and democratic character. Seventeenth century Englishmen first sought to enslave London's beggars and orphans as cheap labor for the Colonies, and then Scotsmen. Finally, Britain shipped 50,000 criminals, rebels, and political outsiders to forced labor in the American Colonies.

Most of these people were sold into a system of indentured servitude. Their numbers were boosted by other whites made so poor and desperate by European economic failure, with its repeated famines and epidemics, that they sold themselves to pay passage for a slim hope of a better life in the Colonies. Nearly half of all colonial immigrants from Britain and Ireland, and seventy percent from Germany, Switzerland, Greece, and Italy, were indentures. They provided nearly all of the cheap labor in early America. They were treated as voluntary slaves – dehumanized, inspected and sold at auction, peddled among plantations and work camps by "soul drivers," and the runaways hounded by bounty hunters.

By the late seventeenth century, Europe had grown wealthier and fewer people had incentive to become indentures. That made indentures expensive. Those bought seemed to their masters lazy, drunken, ungrateful, and far too independent-minded. They wickedly filed lawsuits against their masters for abusive treatment and to protest the harsh legal conditions of their servitude. Too many – about two percent, a figure surprisingly small to a modern viewer but vastly excessive to cost-conscious masters – ran away to backwoods freedom. Ambitious frontier politicians goaded indentures to assert their power and, in 1676, produced Bacon's Rebellion, an uprising of small farmers and indentures against the corruption of a Virginia colonial government dominated by the plantation aristocracy.

As the bulk of the Virginia population was indentured servants and many small farmers were former indentures, Bacon's revolt convinced the colony's elite that indentures were dangerous to keep. These harassed planters looked into the Caribbean to see European colonies grown rich on a system of black slavery that seemed to them cheap and safe. They decided to abandon indentures and copy the Caribbean slave model.

Of the fourteen million Africans kidnapped by European and American slavers or bought from African and Arab slaver traders and hauled to the New World in the years before the British outlawed the Atlantic slave trade in 1807, at least a quarter million were put ashore in North America. The rest were delivered into the more violent Caribbean or the more progressive South American systems. When the U.S. Civil War began, the descendants of those quarter million captives had multiplied to four million people in the United States.[4]

The first Africans were imported into the indenture system with the same legal status and treatment as white indentures. They faced service for a fixed number of years before they achieved freedom to become planters to buy white and black indentures for themselves. However, as the relatively humane indenture system absorbed more slaves, a curious transfer of prejudice took place. The English viewed their own poor as a contemptible and alien race fit only for enslavement in the workhouse. Colonial Englishmen saw white indentures, and their black replacements, as their own alien poor. American race hatred had origins in English class hatred.

African slaves seem to have been realistic about their chances of success in any Spartacus-style uprising, isolated as they were among alien people on an alien continent and with limited means of communication. Slaves who could vanished into the frontier or occasionally joined Indian tribes. Nevertheless, from the beginning of American slavery there were a half dozen serious revolts and many localized rebellions, all violently suppressed.

Contemporary observers – Alexis de Tocqueville, Frederick Law Olmsted, Frederick Douglass, even the comically virulent diehard Confederate writer E. A. Pollard – saw in Southerners a dangerous lack of self-restraint which they ascribed to the savage freedoms of slave ownership. They saw in the South a violent societal atmosphere stemming from the brutality used to discipline slaves, suppress slave revolt, and prevent the ever-expected slave rape of white women. This, they believed, made Southerners hot-tempered and violent. Those attitudes were sustained by a broad illiteracy – nearly half of white Southerners could not read or write in 1860, three times the percentage of Northern illiteracy[5] – which promoted an ignorant suspicion of the foreign and the new.

Escaped slave Frederick Douglass and the abolitionists, exhibiting a romantic assessment of human nature, also saw a moral tension in the South over slavery which they believed drove a readiness for violent action. They were right to a limited degree. The evangelical furor of the Second Great Awakening, which swept the antebellum nation and continued to spurt up during the Civil War (converting generals and regiments on both sides, John Bell Hood among them), drove a moral tension over slavery in the South. However, it seems evident from the contemporary record that much more of any moral tension was the result of stubborn American resistance to outside pressure. In this case, a resistance in the South to a Northern abolitionism propelled by evangelical fervor.

* * *

While these complex developments compounded each other to produce a mid-century regional character that was insular, willfully ignorant of the outside world, and rabidly defensive of any challenge to its slave-holding economy and the white culture that grew out of it, they also produced a surprising civil war within the South. The South rebelled against what it perceived to be the tyranny of its own slaves. The breaking point was the sound of English as spoken by Americans in the South.

European visitors were startled to hear white Southern belles sounding as "black" as their slave housemaids. They reported it with surprise and scorn in best-selling books of their American adventures, shaming white Southerners for their apparent blackness. The South, they seemed to say, is Africa.

English visitors, from ignorance or choice, overlooked the fact that the Southern accent was as much an amalgam of the "dis," "dat," and "fum" working class accent of poor white English men and women who migrated to the South from some parts of southern England as of an African tongue accommodating an alien language. American historian David Hackett Fischer cites The Song of Solomon in a Sussex dialect as "De Song of songs, dat is Solomon's, Let him kiss me wud de kisses of his mouth; for yer love is better dan wine."[6] Some of these sounds are heard still in London's East End and in some backcountry places in England. The accent of the South's blacks and whites meant that a real-life white plantation belle Scarlett O'Hara sounded more like her black slave as portrayed by American actress Butterfly McQueen in the film *Gone With The Wind* than by British actress Vivien Leigh who played Scarlett. "Blackness" was the sound Southern nationalists wanted to exorcise from white mouths.

A Southern nationalism focused on accent would de-Africanize the South and return it to the "Old South" of the eighteenth century when Virginia was the hub of all that was great and good in America, and rich in people, money, and political power. The nineteenth century South saw itself as the nation's defender of the humane values of that glorious past. Of a proper, settled, and unchangeable social and political order. And of the unassailable wealth of the aristocratic, and Southern, few. Purifying the Southern tongue would focus the Southern mind on its ancient glories and fortify the South for its external defense against the economically, demographically, and now politically upstart North.

Southern nationalists preached that the South was spiritually superior to the North. It was more high-toned, cultured, brave, and white. The proof was there in a Puritan yardstick – white Southerners were richer than white Northerners. Southern slave owners had the highest white standard of living in the world, ample proof of Heaven's favor. That calculation ignored, of course, that whites took for themselves all the income generated by the enslaved forty-seven percent of the South's population.

The South saw the North as weirdly out of kilter with a world where most countries at mid-century looked much like the South – rural and agricultural, with repressed labor forces, upward concentrations of wealth, and aristocratic elites determined to keep things that way. The growing wealth of the industrializing North, with its materialistic, democratic, majoritarian, middle-class society, seemed to many in the South as corrupt and corrupting of the national soul, a soul born in the Colonial South.

* * *

The problem for the South was stark. By mid-nineteenth century, the modernizing North was outstripping the South in wealth and population. Southern elites began to see "the tyranny of the majority" robbing them of what they believed rightfully theirs – their traditional ownership of the national government and its protection of slavery. Who could predict what frightfulness lay beyond?

Slave-holders had been the controlling power of the United States for its first seventy-two years, with dominion over the Presidency, Congress, Supreme Court, and the army. The Revolution born in Boston had been won in Virginia by a Virginian, George Washington. The Constitution had rewarded the South with the grant of national leadership in the "three-fifths" gerrymander, counting sixty percent of non-citizen, unenfranchised black slaves into a state's voting population in fixing representation in Congress. Frederick Douglass said it best: "For fifty years the country has taken the law from the lips of an exacting, haughty and imperious slave oligarchy. The masters of slaves have been the master of the Republic."[7]

Now industrialism was producing a progressively richer and healthier environment for a growing number of Northern voters. The North's white live birth rate was higher than the South's. The North's economy attracted a vast number of energetic European immigrants – the South did not want that foreign trash – and a greater number of internal migrants as more white Southerners went north than Northerners went south.

Making matters worse, two generations of regional competition to convert the frontier West into free or slave labor territory ultimately was won by the railroad. Southern elites enriched by their slave-fueled export economy had objected to national improvements that might favor the North. They refused to expand north-south rail links that promised to boost internal trade and increase Northern, as well as Southern, wealth. That compelled the North to turn its railroads, and its thinking, west. The North so heavily colonized what now is the Midwest that the region came to be called "The New North" – a Puritan flower, said Ralph Waldo Emerson, grown in ranker soil. Northern migrants made the West a place of new ideas on power sharing, capitalism, industrial efficiency, and the abolition of slavery.

In good American fashion, the West, under-populated and weak though it was, began to burn with regional hunger for an eventual Western takeover of the national government. In a startling and unhappy development for Southern elites, the parent North chose to cooperate in Western ambition. By demonstrating that it would seek for others what the North expected for itself – a just and democratically won place in a new political order – the North guaranteed that, when war came, the South would have to fight the West, as well. Majority rule was about to overthrow all the South thought the United States Constitution had been designed to protect – Southern hegemony in national government and slavery. The 1860 election of a Northern-minded Westerner, Abraham Lincoln, as President of the United States confirmed for Southern elites the awful problem.

Compounding all these factors, the "old Revolutionary blood" of the first secessionists – the Colonists in 1776 – was still strong in the Civil War generation. It was repeatedly excited by the Latin American wars of liberation against Spain in the first third of the nineteenth century. These fired the imaginations of American youth and Southern fanatics. Agents from every rebel army in the hemisphere swarmed to the U.S. Military Academy at West Point and Southern military schools to recruit mercenary officers to fight the Spanish Empire. Lee refused the offer of a command in South America but others accepted. Their adventures with the great Simon Bolívar and Antonio José de Sucre, Latin American heroes dashing and victorious, confirmed young hearts in the revolutionary spirit. The Southern recruits overlooked the uncomfortable fact that Bolívar believed it madness that any revolution for liberty should maintain slavery.

As the century progressed, the Texan and Cuban independence wars, Europe's 1848 "Year of Revolution," Bleeding Kansas, the Indian Mutiny, Italian Giuseppe Garibaldi fighting for freedom in Brazil, Uruguay, and Italy, Russia's emancipation of the serfs, and the manifestoes of Charles Darwin and Karl Marx quickened in many Americans a yearning for action. It was a revolutionary age and revolution seemed a simple solution to so many complexities in U.S. national politics.

Radicalized Southerners came to believe that preserving slavery and the culture of the South required a United States

enslaved to a dictatorship by Dixie or no United States at all.[8]
Secession had an all-American pedigree dating from 1776.
But no previous secession effort – New England in 1804 pro-
testing the Louisiana Purchase and in 1846 against the Mexican War, Massachusetts in '15 and '44 for commercial
advantage, South Carolina's import tariff nullification in '32
– had been allowed to succeed. It had been evident even to
Southern, slave-holding Presidents that one secession would
lead to many and the death by a thousand cuts for these
united states. That any subdivision of North American
power would invite onto the continent the anti-democrats of
Europe and Asia. No nation is obliged to suffer its own murder nor can a people who had come to imagine for itself a
greatness of character walk away from moral decision. If secession for the sake of slavery had to be made by one side, it
had to be resisted for freedom's sake by the other.

The American nation began to dread and dream of war.
Americans began to see the coming conflict would be about
many things but first about the South's place at the top of the
national pyramid of power and that meant the war would be
about slavery and about the culture determined to protect
slavery.

* * *

CULTURE CHOOSES A MILITARY STRATEGY

The South's political argument for making war – that the election of the incendiary Lincoln forced the region to take the offense in self-defense – was transposed into a national military strategy of the "offensive-defense." The concept was a hybrid of what the South ought to do and what it wanted to do. Southern leadership stuck inflexibly to this strategy from the war's opening at Ft. Sumter, South Carolina, in 1861 to Lee's surrender at Appomattox, Virginia, in 1865 despite the multiple strategy changes made by the North.

The overall offensive-defense concept was the big stall – hold tight to Southern land and resist everywhere to drag out the war to weary the people of the North while raiding their cities to frighten Northern voters into a division of the country. That was a reasonable and potentially successful strategic choice. A strategy that requires time and resilient strength, both of which the Confederacy believed it had in plenty. It also requires national self-control and patience. The Southern population, however, demanded a grand offense-for-defense and not necessarily an offense to support a big stall. Southerners expected their chosen strategy to express foremost their self-assessed fiery national temperament: *Activity! Aggression! Attack!* Drive the war "into Africa" – meaning deep into enemy territory – and raise the victory cheer, urged the *Richmond Enquirer*.[9]

When the cool, complex, time- and land-consuming national strategy of the big stall came into conflict with the self-assessed Southern character of rapid aggression and quick satisfaction, the offense side of the policy won out.

Most Confederate combat commanders worried very little about this philosophical conflict. They ignored their government's national strategy most of the time. They were soldiers hungry to fight and fighting is what they did. "Offense" was for them the operative word in any national military strategy. Robert E. Lee is the foremost example.

Lee stood up publicly for the offensive-defense concept but he was not very good at its military implementation because he liked to fight. The Civil War was a good war for a soldier who had had no stand-up fighting since Mexico, thirteen years before. Lee seems to have enjoyed his Civil War. The challenge of war likely kept alive a man whose failing heart – which may have impaired his command powers at the Battle of Gettysburg – killed him five years after the war's end. Two months before Lee surrendered his beaten army at Appomattox, a Richmond eyewitness wrote in his journal that "Gen. Lee was in the city yesterday, walking about briskly, as if some great event was imminent. His gray locks and beard have become white, but his countenance is cheerful, and his health vigorous."[10] From Abraham Lincoln and Army Commanding General Winfield Scott's offering Lee command of the United States Army at the war's beginning, and by implication the Presidency if Lee scotched secession, through many hot and happy battles to Lee's transcendent moment of soldierly perfection at Appomattox, the thing Lee most loved was battle.

Southerners "had every quality but discipline," said that astute and marvelously arrogant Confederate, Lieutenant General Richard Taylor, son of the former U.S. President Zachary Taylor and former brother-in-law to Jefferson Davis.[11] Lee, the man of famously controlled impulse, could not restrain his hunger to fight, to lead masses of men in desperate combat and to see what happened next. Some saw the strategic senselessness of Lee's approach: "[O]f what earthly use is that 'raid' of Lee's army into Maryland, in violation of all the principles of war?" asked General P. G. T. Beauregard on the first day of the Battle of Gettysburg. "Is it going to end the struggle, take Washington, or save the Mississippi Valley?"[12]

Lee could attack, smash, and make a spectacle to astound the world but he could not find a way to expand his single victories into a war-winning campaign. He could not because he was a war-fighter, not a war-winner. For Lee, national strategy was of little value except as a means to persuade his government to provide him more fighting capacity. But he made the kind of battles mid-century Southern culture expected of him.

For the "Old Army" soldiers like Lee, it had been too long between wars. Their Indian competitors in the West were too good or not good enough. They were bored with peace-time army routine. They wanted a good, big, Napoleonic war. Or just the chance to run howling up Senlac Hill beside Duke William on a bright autumn day in 1066 to go sword against battle-ax with King Harold's best. Most senior Confederate commanders knew an outright military victory on a continental scale was beyond the capacity of the Confederacy. Their political masters could not say that publicly. Many politicians – including Jefferson Davis – may not have realized it. Very few senior commanders, and certainly not Lee, shared in the popular delusion that Europe would intervene for the South to force a political victory. In the meantime, the generals were happy to fight.

To satisfy his soldierly ambition, Lee built one of the greatest armies in United States history – the Army of Northern Virginia – and fought it as though the army had behind it the rich resources of the North, not the poverty of the South. That was his critical error. It caused him to bleed white the South's greatest fighting force. This was a fault common to commanders in a Confederacy whose inept political leadership lacked the conceptual capacity to support its armies with every tool – economic, political, diplomatic, propaganda – necessary to victory. This incapacity in the national authority allowed Lee and other commanders to consider themselves free to be unrestrainedly aggressive. They could power up the offense half of the offensive-defense strategy and answer only to that jolly berserker spirit, thoughtless of consequences, that resides in every soldier and makes soldiering fun. But that is no sure way to win a war.

Jefferson Davis thought to his dying day that the way to beat the North was not an offense-for-defense but a pure defense – stand the ground, rebuff attacks, and wait for world opinion to force the freedom of a victimized Confederacy. European salvation was the persistent dream of Confederate citizens deprived by government censors of the information needed for informed thinking.[13] But Davis's preferred strategy assumed world opinion could be persuaded. It assumed the Northern enemy not clever enough to unpersuade world opinion. It assumed too much more, as well.

A strategy of the long defense requires geographic depth, patience, and nerve – depth into which to retreat in the face of invading armies and enough land and cities to be sacrificed without losing the whole country while persuading the enemy to change its thinking. It requires a population, like Londoners under the 1940-41 German blitz, heroic in their stubborn willingness to suffer as they await the turning point that opens the hour of retribution.

More importantly, it is a strategy that requires generals capable of using strategic depth to the advantage of time and to inflict on the enemy heart the sting of despair. In 1861, the South believed it had all those commodities and a commander of the then-named Confederate Army of the Potomac, Joseph E. Johnston, with a genius for managing the long defense, virtually his only combat capacity as a general. Davis's wearying trap of a long defense combined with a hearts-and-minds strategy might have won for the South as it did for George Washington against the British. But mid-century Southerners refused to make war in a style they considered passive. A pure defense was culturally unacceptable. The idea was shoved aside.

Instead, the South selected a national strategy – the of-fensive-defense – it was not equipped to make succeed and a strategy that allowed its generals the freedom to squander resources needed for success. The South did that, in part, because Southerners, as Northerners, had forgotten the reality of war. Frontier skirmishes with the Indians aside, the country's last war was with Mexico over the possession of Texas, 1846-48. That war filled the newspapers and the national imagination with exotic landscapes and people and wild victories. But it had been fought far away by profession-als and adventurers, not by men and boys pulled from every village in the land. No American towns were torched, few coffins went home to country crossroads, no monuments were raised to Our Mexican War Dead, the now-fabled Al-amo was left to rot. It had been war against a Mexican army so professional, so well equipped, so European in style that the man who had beaten Napoleon – the Duke of Wellington – expected Mexico to whip the rag-tag ex-Colonials in double quick-time.

By 1860, most of those Americans who had fought in Mexico seem to have forgotten the frightfulness of that war. Of fields strewn with arms, legs, and heads. Of towns and farm fields the work of generations blown away. Of women raped, children starved, disease rampant. Of the burden of caring for lurching veteran cripples and a national treasury sunk in debt. Without that memory, the people of the South let themselves be goaded on by Southern fanatics and ambitious politicians. These propagandized the Southern people that, contrary to the lessons of history, victory could be bought fast and cheap with nothing more than style, heart, and will, if necessary. They forgot that their chosen enemy had plenty of those commodities, too, and a good deal more the South did not have.

Northern manpower resources were five-to-two greater than the South's, the North had ten times as many industrial workers as the South, twice the railroads and three times the draft animals, ninety-six percent of the nation's locomotives, and ninety-seven percent of its firearms. Most of the U.S. Navy's ships stayed with the Union. The North had almost all of the country's mechanized agriculture and far out-produced the food harvests of the South. Southern agriculture was devoted to export crops – tobacco, sugar, cotton. The war consumed half of Northern industrial output. The mass organization and standardization imposed on industry by the war's demands converted Northern businesses into large, efficient, dynamically expansive operations able to stand behind an army, navy, and government growing equally large, efficient, and dynamic. A young officer in the Army of the Potomac wrote in wonder about "my country, hardly feeling this draft upon its resources, and growing richer every day."[14] The war made the North modern and rich, richer when the war ended than when it began.

Southern strategists and commanders relied on a unique resource to balance Northern material superiority – the Southern fighting spirit. Meaning a cold-blooded calculation of the willingness of Confederate soldiers to suffer casualties disproportionate to the enemy and to the value of any one victory that could be achieved. One statistic tells the story: A soldier in gray had a thirty percent chance of dying in combat or of wounds, disease, and general misery while a soldier in blue faced half that risk.[15]

Readiness to sacrifice themselves gave gray soldiers a hell-raising capacity out of proportion to the size of their fighting units. It allowed Confederate strategists and generals to push hungry, ragged, shoeless men into unnecessarily desperate actions in which self-sacrifice was the key to winning. Pickett's great frontal charge at Gettysburg uphill against a stone wall lined with too many Northern riflemen and artillery pieces failed not because too few Confederate soldiers were ready to die for their cause on that ghastly July afternoon in 1863 but because Lee did not put enough of them into the kill zone. Nor did Jefferson Davis that night wander his presidential mansion weeping for his lost legions.

Southern spirit was the first and the last coin of Confederate military strategy. It gave the South three years of victories, until 1864 when commanders arose in the North ready to apply a new method to the Union's war-fighting and produced the war of logistics that remains today the trademark of U.S. military strategy.

The logistics war grew out of the power of the undersized but exceptionally hell-raising gray armies to frustrate Federal ambitions in head-to-head fighting. Northern strategists saw they had to find an indirect means to break those armies. Politicians and publics North and South yearned for decisive, storybook battles of annihilation. But the experience of marching through Old Mexico with Winfield Scott's little army had taught generals blue and gray to expect a more prosaic war. A war of progressively faster grinding away of the weakest underpinnings of the two war machines – material supports in the South and public opinion in the North – until whichever side ground fastest won. "Hard pounding, gentlemen," Wellington ordered his captains as they looked across the field of Waterloo at Napoleon's gathering legions, and, "we will see who can pound the longest." Grinding away became the fighting style that dominated American strategic thinking until the arrival of nuclear weapons and stealth technologies a century later.

* * *

To undergird the South's offensive-defense strategy and to draw in European military support, the South believed it had the equivalent of a nuclear weapon in cotton. Jefferson Davis and his government, in a kind of principled blackmail, held Southern cotton off the world market to force Europeans to wake to the moral necessity of staking European lives, fortunes, and sacred honor on the Confederate cause.

In dollar, pound, and franc terms, this seemed a clever calculation. A good many Northern businessmen agreed and, foreseeing the loss of cotton exports throttling the national economy, wanted the war to end before it ruined American business.[16] Textile production provided all or part of the livelihood for nearly twenty percent of the British population. Cotton was the industry's mainstay. Ninety-two percent of Britain's cotton imports in 1860 – one billion pounds of it – came from the United States. Embargo the South's cotton exports to close down the vast textile and associated industries and British working men and women with their children in the tens of thousands would starve and turn to riot and rebellion against their own government. European kings and parliaments, already sympathetic with the Southern cause, would be forced in self-defense to join the South and internationalize the Confederate war by sending European armies and navies to fight the North.

But Davis and those very many in the South who supported this scheme were wrong in their calculation because war never is simply about dollars, pounds, and francs. It also is about spirit and character and sometimes about the driving direction of the world. Strange that a revolution which claimed to be about passionate conviction of the right would think another people could have so little self-respect as to be blackmailed into joining a foreign war that had no existential importance for them. Yet that is what Davis and much of the South believed. That low estimate of the European character offended the same kings and aristocrats inclined to support the South and they refused to be blackmailed. But that was only part of the story.

Davis was doubly wrong in seeking to use cotton as a goad because he misjudged the world's economic direction. He did so because he was oddly ignorant of the workings of capitalism, another reflection of parochial Southern thinking at mid-century. Efficiencies in the use of Eli Whitney's cotton gin cut the market price of cotton by one-third, driving down the cost of a fabric that once was a luxury good to a level the common man could afford. Cotton was easier to produce and easier to work into textiles than linen or wool. These factors made cotton, in historian Paul Johnson's view, "probably the most valuable agricultural staple in the world" after 1815.[17] It is true there was precedent in American Colonial times for a product embargo to move Europe politically. But there also was precedent for an embargo invigorating alternative products. U.S. trade embargoes from 1807 to 1815, spanning the Napoleonic wars, drove the North to develop its industries such that, by 1860, Northern rather than British mills supplied most U.S. consumption of finished cotton. The Confederacy overlooked the risk of this happening on an international scale.

Further, Davis and his cohort had failed to do some fundamental arithmetic. The South had not bothered to track sales against consumption to discover that a foresighted Europe had an eighteen months' supply of cotton stuffed in its warehouses. Those British textile makers so dependent on cheap cotton could afford to wait a very long while before being forced to consider committing lives, honor, fortune to any sort of action.

When that moment for commitment finally arrived, English textile makers demonstrated two more things the South had overlooked. First, capitalism is infinitely flexible. In any crisis, it will seek an alternative route to product and profit. Britain consumed 80 percent of Southern cotton production. But, when the South embargoed its cotton, British capitalism turned to Indian and Egyptian cotton and set up the Australian cotton industry. Capitalism made blockade-run exports from Dixie unnecessary.

Second, the British ruling class discovered that an excess of democracy had robbed them of the pleasure to make war at whim. The British Parliament at the middle of the nineteenth century was filled with America-hating conservatives still dissatisfied with the results of 1776. British elites, as Northern businessmen, saw slavery as a necessary evil to the production of cheap cloth and high profits. It was convenient to let what they saw as the touchy, noisy, and too rich troglodyte planters of the South shoulder alone the moral blame for slavery. But, as Calvin Stowe in 1853 told Londoners outraged at his insolence, the abolisher of the Atlantic slave trade had the power to end American slavery overnight by refusing to buy Southern cotton. That complicity stung the hearts of the five million English men and women with their children – one-fifth of the nation – working in the textile industry.[18] The moral awakening of Americans in the early nineteenth century had been preceded by an awakening of Englishmen, and these ordinary working men and women who in Britain had not yet won the right to vote saw the Confederate war for slavery as immoral and a threat to free labor and democratic progress for English working people. They became partisans for the North, preferring to starve than work slave-grown cotton. Their public demonstrations told Parliament that to intervene for the slave South could add civil war at home to a trans-Atlantic war with the free North. They kept Britain neutral.

A further problem for Britain, and that meant for Confederate hopes of European intervention, was Russia. France wanted even more than Britain to join for the South but France and Britain feared that sending military forces to

Dixie would so weaken European security as to invite re-newed, post-Crimean War Russian adventurism. Although Russia had abolished serfdom in 1860 to raise happier troops for more czarist misadventure, it had no interest in the American argument over slavery. Russia wanted to preserve the U.S. as a counterbalance to British power and to satisfy Russia's eternal craving for access to warm water ports. Rus-sia wanted to make war on Japan and the rump United States offered safe harbors for wintering the Imperial Russian Navy. The Union had no interest in joining Russia's Pacific adventures, although the U.S. fought and won a naval battle against the Japanese in 1863.[19] But the North wanted Britain and France to see Russian spars on the skylines of San Fran-cisco and New York. Czarist sailors on shore leave in the fleshpots of the Bowery and the Barbary Coast helped to pre-vent a world war for cotton.

Even if America-hating British and French elites ignored all these problems, how were Britain and France to get their regiments onto American soil past the world's most power-ful and modern navy, the U.S. Navy? And if they managed to put their soldiers alongside Confederate troops and botched fighting the world's most powerful and modern army, the U.S. Army, what would the United States do in revenge – take Canada from Britain and chase the French out of Mexico and the Caribbean?

The British elite, with no financial need to support the South, looked at all these problems and decided it had no domestic or European political need, either. As Sun Tzu, aphorist-in-chief of the modern U.S. military, says, "Before you fight, count the cost." Europe counted the cost to win the war for the South and found it too high. There would be no world war for cotton.

Jefferson Davis and the Southern majority that agreed with him made these miscalculations of European intent out of a misreading of the world's reality born from cultural insularity. If "Confederate faith," steadfast principle, and hot passion meant Davis measured up to the ideal of Southern character at mid-century, those qualities were all he had. He was a self-proclaimed revolutionary leader blind to the direction of a revolutionary century. The world was moving away from its ancient institutions of princes and slaves and toward the common man of whatever color supported by capitalism and opportunity. Davis and most in the South would not accept that change. The North, despite its own debilitating misperceptions, made itself part of the century's flow. The South would not.

* * *

CULTURE CHOOSES A GENERAL

John Bell Hood had the bigness Americans then and now expect in their heroes – nearly six feet tall, two hundred pounds, and fair-eyed, fair-haired, raw-boned as a back-woodsman, and hot and eager as an Indian brave. He also had in him the boyishness Americans want in a hero – he blushed at hearing the name of the girl he loved, whichever girl that happened to be at the moment. To the people of his time, Hood seemed a cavalier out of legend, lively, hearty, brave, a war-lover. He had been raised to join the slave-holding aristocracy of the South and made Robert E. Lee his model as gentleman, aristocrat, and general. At thirty-three in 1864, Hood became the youngest full general in the Confederate States Army and a battered hero of some of the war's bloodiest battlefields.

Men who knew him thought Hood a man's man. It is easy to imagine him, just as the old stories tell, full of masculine good cheer on the deck of a steamboat or in a tavern or at the campfire, a raucous drinking buddy full of tales of his adventures fighting Indians in Texas, a man who would bet a thousand dollars – two years' pay for a young cavalry lieutenant – on the turn of a card. He was brave and strong and fist-fought his private soldiers for discipline, and so what if he cuffed his slaves and servants and a speech defect made "Calolina" from "Carolina." He was conventionally religious, a conventional slave man who expected slave-made wealth to propel him up the social ladder, and a conventional racist. He did not think about too much.

Women who knew him saw Hood as a romantic figure, dashing, exciting, and boyish, a master of the dramatic flourish in combat but a tongue-tied and charming stumbler in what his century called "love making." Women can be attracted to power and aggression and the women of the South were strongly attracted to Hood because they themselves were outstandingly aggressive for the rebel Cause. "I could not love you," a Southern woman told her own soldier, "if you had stayed at home content to remain inactive at such a moment."[20]

Reading the contemporary record, including his curiously named memoir *Advance and Retreat*, shows Hood to have been impulsive and passionate, a man for whom the war was a ferocious and happy outlet. Combat demanded just the qualities he possessed, transforming Hood from a limited young man with a limited future into a warrior who, with a bit of luck, might out-stonewall Stonewall Jackson to become his nation's premier combat hero.

War politics and the newspapers then shaped Hood into an exemplar of the resentful and resisting South standing heroically against a new and modernizing world. That opened for him astonishing political possibilities beyond the ordinary expectations of a boy from a Huckleberry Finn wilderness. Win the war with Lee and Hood might take the prize traditionally offered war-winning American generals – the presidency of his country, after Lee. Across the combat frontier, that same dream was being offered to battle-winning Union Generals Grant and Sherman.

But there was a curious defect in Hood as general, politician, friend or lover that made him a lonely and a lonesome man. Retired to his tent or in the glitter of the Confederate president's wife's salon, Hood was a hero without that ordinary substance that invites friendship. Such a want may seem a small thing as generals are chosen to win, not to be loved. But Hood's story is that of a simple man made complex by war, of an ordinary man made strange, of a lonely man made the welcome hero, of a mid-century Southern man expected to save a nation that had too few of the tools necessary for him to do the work.

* * *

Hood was born on June 29, 1831, in Kentucky, a few steps higher up the social ladder than his fellow Kentuckians Abraham Lincoln and Jefferson Davis. Lincoln, who became President of the United States, was born into what he himself called white trash. Davis, the Confederate president, was born in the first cabin in his village with glass windows. Hood's family came from better stock. They were not roving subsistence farmers, as the Lincolns and most other pioneers who used up and abandoned the land and moved on, setting the foundations for our throw-away culture. The Hoods were a stable tribe, literate if not educated, certain in their belief that more land and more slaves to work the land was the way to the riches that would allow them to climb into the Southern aristocracy.

Hood's father, Dr. John Hood, was a medical quack with a bizarre mechanical solution to disease and not much to recommend him as a parent. He found himself a wife who brought him 225,000 acres of mountain land and who had the skill to manage it for him. That was a good thing for the family's survival as the doctor was consumed by his belief that disease results from a disarrangement of the body's internal organs. He believed he alone had the cure – in patent metal, bone, and leather corsets that would shove, squeeze and pinch the organs into their correct positions, as assessed by Dr. Hood.

Print advertisements of the period show his corset designs to be as ingenious as any instrument of torture devised for the Spanish Inquisition. But, in an age before acceptance of the germ theory, this solution seemed to some patients as reasonable as any other. These contrivances may have worked with a convincing frequency as Dr. Hood became guru to a group of Philadelphia medical students happy to outrage the local medical establishment in academic combat over Dr. Hood's theory. Or perhaps these students merely saw the rich commercial possibilities in medical corsets.

Income from Dr. Hood's medicine, his teaching each academic year in Philadelphia, and his wife's slave-based farming provided his three sons a life sufficiently stable and rich that they, unlike most other boys and girls in that age, were exempt from the sweat of daily farm labor. Young Abe Lincoln, who despised the drudgery of farming and almost seems to have made himself President to escape it forever, would have envied them.

Hood was free to live the half-wild life of a boy growing up in that idyllic existence that is at the heart of the American myth, of the boy roaming the Indian-haunted forests, hunting, fishing, and dreaming in youth's endless summertime, with the cocky and self-assured character we Americans claim as our style. Hood won a reputation as a village troublemaker, a fist-fighter, and leader of boys' pranks. He was a spoiled member of a grubby frontier elite buying its way up the social ladder, in good American fashion.

But his father's absence from home for much of each academic year, selling his theories or his frauds, seems to have marked Hood deeply. That is to be seen in his relationship with Robert E. Lee, another father-abandoned child and one who made sons of his soldiers. And in the crippled war hero's careful nursing his wife and eldest daughter stricken with yellow fever in an abandoned New Orleans in 1879, until Hood himself was stricken and died.

Despite the advantages of literacy and Dr. Hood's academic life in Philadelphia, there is little evidence the doctor's family was much aware of the greater currents reworking American life. Of Nathaniel Hawthorne, Ralph Waldo Emerson, and Edgar Allan Poe. Of Samuel Morse's electric telegraph and the newly popular game of "base ball." Of the energetic reshaping of Northern cities and the building of the West by the railroads. They must have heard of Uncle Tom's Cabin and probably read some Charles Dickens. But, on their plantations, the family seems to have been little touched by what to others was an age of astonishing change – steam engines replacing man- and horse-power, early feminism, a globalizing economy, the revolt of the oppressed in many distant places, of the common man muscling his way forward to become the driving force of the West. That common man came in a variety of skin colors in Europe and so, too, he must in the North and South.

What the Hood family did know was religious revivalism – though Hood's mother appears to have raised him a conventional Baptist – along with the frightfulness of Nat Turner's slave uprising in 1831 and the glamour of revolution in Texas from 1836. But their advantages made the family only slightly less isolated from the world outside their farmlands than other pioneering families. And they were part of a South that was increasingly suspicious and resentful of what was not itself.

* * *

Hood was a lucky man and would be a lucky soldier and, so long as his luck held out, he was a winner for the South.

But none of that was apparent in the ordinary fellow Hood seemed to be when he showed up at the U.S. Military Academy at West Point, New York, in 1849. His uncle, a Congressman, got him the appointment.

Southern cadets generally made a poorer academic showing at West Point than Northern cadets. Southern white children spent half as many days in school as did Northern children, fewer even than children in the pioneer West. In an early affirmative action program, entrance requirements to the Point were kept low to enable Southern boys to be admitted. Hood nearly was expelled for unruly conduct and poor grades. Library records show he checked out only one book in his four years at the Point.

Hood studied Jominian strategy under the great Dennis Hart Mahan who emphasized to the cadets aggressiveness and massed Napoleonic attacks. Beyond the idea of attack, there is no evidence Mahan's teaching – or Napoleon, for that matter – made much impression on Hood. He was "daring and reckless, though not over-talented," his West Point roommate, Union Major General John M. Schofield, wrote after the war.[21] Schofield and other cadets saved Hood's Academy career by tutoring him afterhours. Hood graduated forty-fourth out of a class of fifty-two. The Northerner George Armstrong Custer did worse – anchorman of the class of '61 – but made brigadier general younger, at age twenty-three.

With his brand-new gold epaulettes, Second Lieutenant John Bell Hood was sent to dreary outposts in California, the lonely places that drove Captain Ulysses S. Grant to drink. Hood's meager army pay made him a poor man in Gold Rush California. But Hood farmed and sold his produce to the gold miners at the customary exorbitant prices. Then he was posted to Texas and Hood's military adventure began.

Texas was a marvel of wildness and beauty that appealed to Hood's spirit. Serene plains and mountains, the shifting colors of the desert, dark-eyed and teasing mixed-blood women, the smoke and glitter of Catholic ceremonies in antique churches, Sam Houston's "Texian" veterans with their gaudy war stories, planters with their grand money-making schemes based on importing 200,000 slaves, and exotic Old Mexico just over the horizon. Hood found a broad new scope for his unfocused ambitions. But he did not seem to understand the new professional territory – the responsibility of military command – into which he had drifted.

While the actions of a junior officer normally should not be read to judge those of the experienced and mature man risen to high command, the greatest event of Lieutenant Hood's career on the Texas-Indian borderline is too much like his great moments in the Civil War to be overlooked. On July 5, 1857, Hood led twenty-five troopers and an Indian scout of Company G, 2nd U.S. Cavalry – Major George H. Thomas, acting regimental commander – on an epic 150 mile pursuit of a Comanche war party that outnumbered his force two to one. They took thirty days' rations and rode bravely into the wasteland.

The expedition became a hard slog across a boiling desolation. Troopers exhausted, horses crippled, water supplies nearly gone, Hood on July 18 finally spotted his quarry at a place unhappily named Devil's River. In his enthusiasm for battle, Hood led his men into an ambush. Into desperate hand-to-hand, muzzle-in-the-face fighting, the fields around them set ablaze by the Comanches. Hood saw his men being whipped and ordered a fighting retreat, with two dead and four severely wounded, Hood's hand tacked to his bridle by an arrow.

This was Hood's first field command and his first combat engagement. He had shown himself brave, aggressive, rash, and thoughtless. He wasted the lives of two troopers by not finishing the job in annihilating the war party or compelling them to submit. He merely had a good brawl, a boy's adventure in a John Ford landscape. He loved it.

From this event to Hood's assumption of command of the Confederate Army of Tennessee seven years later there is surprisingly little maturing to be seen in Hood. He was given no intermediate seasoning in unit management and command between his time as a lieutenant in Texas and his appointment in 1861 as a major in the Confederate States Army. The old U.S. Army of 26,000 officers and men was too small to allow Hood much scope for advancement except across a very long time period. The new Confederate forces needed even his limited military training and experience too badly to grant him the leisure to learn a major's job. Military organizations assembled on the run to their first battles generally expect young officers appointed more or less blindly to mid-grade command to succeed in their first combats or be killed off to save the bother of cashiering them.

Hood moved from a callow but very confident junior officer in blue, most of whose military decisions were made for him by his superiors, to a not much more thoughtful but supremely confident field grade officer in gray who was expected to make a good many critical decisions.

Despite his defect in military seasoning, Hood flourished in the new Confederate armed forces because he showed the marks of a hero and a winner. That was enough for his soldiers to love him, despite his mismanagement of their supply and their lack of sufficient shoes, tents, good meat, axle grease. Hood's disdain for logistics was partly hidden in the general chaos of the gray army's early days and in its warlong poverty. What Hood was good at was winning fights and that was what his soldiers loved about him.

If Hood repeatedly used direct assaults that cost a lot of soldier lives, he also made victories for his troops. In the beginning, there was not much more he could do with the amateurs who were his troops. Herding his soldiers into frontal assaults was about as much as he could manage.

The only thing a soldier likes more than a general who wins victories is a general who wins victories the soldier can survive. Hood found a way to help his soldiers survive. He taught them to fire as they ran in the attack, an innovation that gave each soldier more confidence in his own survival. Sometimes, of course, Hood drove his men so fast they had no time to fire but just enough time to reach the enemy parapet, climb over it, and shout for the enemy to surrender. That, too, was survivable victory. The soldier could be happy about it and proud of his general.

Hood also made assault his primary tactic because the Southern newspapers loved attack and loved him for making attacks. And because Robert E. Lee gave him no other work to do in the Army of Northern Virginia. Hood's foot charge won Gaines's Mill for Lee and Hood's charge stopped Hooker's division at Antietam for Lee. Hood led his assaults personally – not just because that was expected of a commander in that age, but because Hood loved aggression.

* * *

Without his uniform, John Bell Hood might have made little more of his life than did his two brothers, one a wastrel and the other a poor silver miner and wandering preacher, neither of whom seems to have served the Confederacy in combat. But the Civil War came, and no other officer in the Confederate States Army was promoted more rapidly to full general – from cavalry lieutenant in blue to army commander in gray in three years. Very few other men won their general's stars by such a profitable coincidence of heroism, political connections, and accident. Very few others so fully met the requirements of the culture from which they sprang to leadership. Hood had a heroic spirit on a mythic scale that mid-century Southern culture demanded of its men. This quality appears to have blotted out his military inexperience and command inadequacy for many in his national leadership until they promoted him beyond his capacity.

In the age of the *Follow Me* combat leader, Hood was more "follow me" than anyone else in Confederate gray. In Union blue, his only comparable was Custer who, eleven years after the Civil War, led his 7th Cavalry into catastrophe in an Indian ambush. Hood had the berserker spirit of the antique warrior. He was courageous, daring, charismatic, unrelenting, and thoughtless of self. A war-lover. Hood and his Texas Brigade, his first great command, made themselves into the attack dogs of the Army of Northern Virginia. Lee employed Hood as Supreme Allied Commander Dwight Eisenhower used Lieutenant General George Patton in World War II – *Go out there,* Ike would say to Georgie, *and smash them!* That is what Hood would do for Lee – he would smash them. Hood was the kind of general whom a frightened, dirty, shoeless soldier could be proud to call his own and willingly follow.

Hood's military career in the Confederate States Army was the charmed climb up the ladder of success that any officer would prefer to the usual drudgery of learning the trade on dreary backcountry outposts and being tested at each incremental step up in command. When he signed on with the Confederate States Army, Hood was immediately promoted from Federal lieutenant to Confederate major because he was Old Army and available. He was made brigadier general as part of a political package to advance a friend of Jefferson Davis.

Hood's fame began with his dynamic command of the Texas Brigade, some of its troops the tough frontiersmen who had fought in the Mexican War of 1846-48. But the brigade was given him largely by default. Lee wanted to use Hood and Lone Star State political influence to expand his own Army of Northern Virginia. He called for a second Texas brigade to be built around Hood and given to Lee's army. When Brigadier General Louis T. Wigfall, Hood's patron and father of his girlfriend-of-the-moment – one in a series of rich, well-connected young women – traded his command of the original Texas Brigade for a seat in the Confederate congress, Lee found he had cornered himself into awarding Wigfall's brigade to Hood.

Lee botched the battle of Antietam. Hood and the Texas Brigade saved him from disaster. Lee understood national and army politics and smart public relations and made Hood a major general. Lee also understood the limitations of this boy-general and gave Hood command of the Army of Northern Virginia's lightest division, 7,000 men. The record of the war suggests Lee thought Hood's lack of seasoning along his meteoric rise meant Hood needed tight controlling. But Hood showed himself a good division commander if a bad logistician, an intelligent and charismatic manager of men, a clever tactician and perceptive strategist, and a man who could move a large force with elegance and speed. He was a commander who, within Lee's ensemble, could succeed.

Hood made his next leap – promotion to lieutenant general – in Varina Davis's salon. There her husband, the Confederate president, decided to position Hood to succeed his bitterest political enemy in uniform – Joseph E. Johnston – as commander of the great and often rebellious Army of Tennessee.

But there was a good deal more to Hood's last few steps up the promotion ladder than politics and enmity. The most important, most curious, most human factor is that Jefferson Davis believed in Hood. Davis was ready to bet the war, the Confederacy, and his own neck on Hood because Davis recognized in him a man genuinely willing to die for the Cause. A true last-ditcher. And because this half-blind, sour, and impatient old man Jeff Davis once had been a wild young Louisiana Rifleman hurrahing across the exotic landscape of Mexico, who preferred his boot-stomping dances with sloe-eyed, half-breed girls and rode half-broken ponies, and who eloped with Sarah Knox Taylor, daughter of his Mexican War commander and later President, Zachary Taylor. Davis took Sarah to his remote Mississippi plantation where, within a few months of their marriage, she died of malaria. He sank into a hard-edged gloom that seems never to have left him, even after his second marriage. But Hood, heroic and adventurous, made that young Rifleman come alive again within Davis. The president had to have this war-mad cowboy to general his last great army.

* * *

The Marble Model and a Confederate Princess

This portrait of Hood as a frontier boy raised toward the Southern slave-aristocracy and elevated, despite inadequate seasoning, to a general's stars and then shaped by Confederate newspapers and government propaganda into the avatar of a bloody-handed hero is incomplete without understanding the impact on his life of Robert E. Lee and Sarah "Buck" Campbell Buchanan Preston.

Lee came first into Hood's life. Hood was trained by Lee at West Point, seasoned by Lee in Texas, and raised up by Lee in Virginia. Hood made all of his successes in Lee's Army of Northern Virginia. He modeled himself on the older general. But Hood seems to have learned only from Lee's savage aggressiveness and failed to realize that the "king of spades"

was a battlefield conservative with, as historian Harold Se-
lesky of the University of Alabama likes to say, the instincts
of a riverboat gambler. Lee knew when to dig holes in the
ground from which to fight and when to take a running
chance. He took his chances when he saw them and some,
as at Antietam, are hair-raising when outlined on a map. Lee
grew accustomed to beating risks that would have destroyed
another commander. That remains the foundation of his
reputation.

But Lee's conduct in battle and in his home life leads to
the unsettling conclusion that he was a bloodthirsty, and
perhaps manic-depressive, fighting man who believed that
any fight is better than no fight at all. Hood responded pow-
erfully to this wildness in Lee and did so because the two
were much alike: Two father-abandoned, female-flum-
moxed personalities whose dynamism was damped in ordinary peacetime but who were freed by war to be the hottest
of brawlers.

Yet Lee at Fredericksburg, staring down from Marye's
Heights at the churning red horror his artillery was making
of Federal troops – 10,000 dead in an afternoon – said to his
"Old War Horse" Lieutenant General James Longstreet, "It is
well that war is so terrible, or we should grow too fond of
it."[22] The customary reading of that line says there on the
Heights the great Lee saw himself and humankind with a
harsh, ironic clarity. But there also is a lip-smacking awful-
ness in what he said that stings the heart with fright. Here

lies the difference between Lee and Hood – Hood never had a Marye's Heights moment. He seems never to have looked inside himself at all.

Lee used Hood ruthlessly as the power punch to break the enemy's front line. At Gaines's Mill on June 27, 1862, Hood, possessed – according to soldiers' accounts – by a battle mania, personally led his Texans in the foot charge up Turkey Hill that broke the Federal line Lee had been unable to penetrate any other way. Hood and his soldiers ran uphill and through water into the flame and iron of artillery firing downslope. Although Hood had trained his troops to fire on the run, a shocking innovation to blue soldiers facing those gray muzzles, Hood's Texans cleared away their enemies with a charge so fast they had no time to shoot. Hood captured a New Jersey regiment and lost twenty-nine percent of his troops. Every officer above the rank of captain was killed. Hood's Texas Brigade with Evander M. Law's brigade of Georgians charging alongside lost 1,016 men in less than an hour. But Hood won the battle for Lee. The victory at Gaines's Mill was Hood's greatest combat achievement. Then, at Antietam on September 17, 1862, his division counterattacked "Fighting Joe" Hooker's Federal corps and threw it back, taking fifty percent losses but preserving the Rebel left flank. When the fighting was over, Hood's division was wrecked.

This was a war in which men and not machines did the manful work, in which physical endurance and character counted for more than equipment or fighting machines. To watch Hood's division charging through flying metal with men shot away in hundreds on all sides, the survivors enduring in a few minutes more threat and horror than most men and women are offered in the full span of ordinary life, is to marvel at what the charisma of one raw, half-trained general can lead men to do.

Lee always made good use of Hood but the tasks Lee gave Hood, and the units he assigned the young general, show clearly that Lee knew Hood's limits as well as his abilities. Hood lacked the intellectual capacity to observe and to understand how Lee used him and, more importantly, how Lee managed a battle. Reviewing the historical record also makes apparent that Lee lacked the capacity to educate a man such as Hood in good battle management. That failure was Lee's contribution to the debacle that Hood made in 1864.

Lee treated his generals like his sons but none proved successful away from Lee's military family, Lee's own army. Even Longstreet, a superior strategist and general, floundered when he tried a command independent of Lee. Lee, like Napoleon, could train up able lieutenants but he was incapable of making them independent leaders. He raised daughters who would not marry and could not be happy away from him. He raised up generals who could not succeed except in the leadership ensemble he had created for the army he loved.

* * *

By 1863 and risen to command a division in Longstreet's corps of Lee's Army of Northern Virginia, Hood had a heroic reputation to uphold and vast new opportunity on his horizon. He needed to snare as his wife a rich, politically well-connected young woman to boost him toward his bright ambition. In that, Hood was following his family's expectation for him. Nor was he acting any differently to his fellow Kentuckian, Abraham Lincoln, who married rich and up the social ladder to boost his political prospects.

But Hood was without any wife-prospects at the moment. He had thrown over pretty Louise Wigfall when her father fell out of favor with Hood's newest patron, Jefferson Davis. So in March, while Hood still was physically whole and as Lee reorganized his army for the invasion of Pennsylvania that would end in disaster at Gettysburg, Hood went into Richmond to shop for a wife.

Richmond, the Confederate capital, was no cosmopolis. It was a jumped up country town decorated by Thomas Jefferson and made rich by slave-grown tobacco and cotton. A city small even by contemporary Southern standards. Stuffed with the ambitious, the social-climbing, and the war-profiteering for whom the double risk of losing the war and facing a hangman's noose for treason meant they must live life at a desperate pace. These people made Richmond electric with nerve, hope, and fright. Too many men and women were hungry for everything because tomorrow might not be another day. Tomorrow could be ruin and desolation but the flesh is now. Richmond was a city hot with tumbling sex.

Those more confident in the war's success, such as Hood, could ignore the frenzy around them and prospect for old-fashioned love, marriage, and a rich dowry. For fashionable virgins, the frenzied atmosphere meant even more grand fun teasing at love and watching the golden boys twist on their golden hooks. Into this hothouse environment would come, like a comet shooting out of space, some gray and red hero to drive all other fevers to new excitement. Best if this comet were a general and better still a victorious general. If not definitely victorious, then patriotically wounded. But if a failure, then a general with a smoldering excitement in his eye that threatened to bring down the temple. This frenzied little community would lionize him because he was all the distraction they had at the moment. They would send him back on campaign fortified with some of what they had to give – their desperate hopes, their fear of a Northern noose, their social-climbing and war-profiteering ambitions, their sexual energies, and their gift of celebrity.

In this electric environment, Hood applied himself to his love making with a stubborn determination and social clumsiness that amused many. His antics became jolly parlor stories passed around Richmond. The planter and political families that could decide a young man's future thought him comically inept at anything not to do with fighting Yankees. They made Hood the centerpiece of their grand fetes – first as the heroic boy general and later as the great commander made available to them by patriotic wounds – because he amused them. Society laughed to find Hood barely able to hold his own in polite conversation – had he read nothing, met no one, been nowhere, made no money? – and snickered to find the blood-red hero a blushing stammerer before the charge of crinolined young women. His West Point training was no use in this social combat – the Point was no finishing school, especially for a young man who avoided its library. Hood stumbled and pawed across the social landscape, only half aware of the frightful scene he was making and perhaps too self-inflated to understand much of it.

Hood met Mary and Buck Preston – "Buck" for her exploits on horseback – at the house of the Civil War's most famous gossip, Mary Chesnut. The sisters were rich, attractive, and politically well-connected. Their father made his fortune planting sugar in Louisiana, a state infamous for its abuse of slaves and for seeking extra profit in working them to death to replace with fresh imports, on the Caribbean rather than mainland model. He was chief of the powerful Conscription Bureau, assessed by some historians as the most corrupt agency in the Confederate government. Preston's fortune allowed him to travel to Europe to collect romantic art and to send his daughters to Europe for some part of their education. His wife was the sister of Major General Wade Hampton, Lee's cavalry commander. The Federal capture of New Orleans, Louisiana, in 1862 would have ruined Preston but for money he had stashed in Europe and more held in trust for him by Union Major General Ambrose E. Burnside. Preston told Burnside to keep the money until the war was over as it seemed "safer in Burnside's hands" than his own.[23] The Confederacy might be swept away by blue power but the reverse was unlikely even after a gray victory. This was a sensible precaution but smacks of betting against your country.

Hood first targeted Mary Preston, the livelier older sister. Men always seemed to go for her first. Buck remained in the background, silent, sullen, pouty, and more alluring for being the mysterious presence in her sister's shadow. Twenty-year old Buck gradually drew Hood's attention away from Mary. She was not Charlotte Temple, the simpering ball-cutter of the namesake novel of the early Republic, nor the venal and selfish Scarlett O'Hara. She was both, and in spades. Buck also had about her a strange ill luck for those fascinated by her – each of five successive suitors was killed in combat or in duels before she met Hood. Mary Chesnut's brother, himself half in love with Buck, began to warn men it was safer to face a Union battery than to fall in love with Buck Preston.[24] Hood fell hopelessly – no, better to say drunkenly – in love with a Southern belle who now used and abused him with an energy and imagination to make Scarlett O'Hara blush. This ladder-climbing young cynic had succumbed to true love.

There are some male historians, perhaps wrapped up in their own romance for Buck, who suspect her alternately welcoming and rejecting Hood showed she did not know her own mind about loving him. There are some female historians, perhaps reflecting a different bias, who suspect she was a rebel against the restrictions of conventional female life in her time. More likely, the Preston family wealth and position gave Buck the luxury to continue to act like a feckless teenager into her twenties. She played a child's game of life: She could love Hood and not love Hood all at once, as she loved and did not love all of the other marvelous young men who swarmed around her and her sister. When the young men were not there, her languid, public melodrama of pining for lovers happily *in absentia* inspired others to pet and fret over her and that kept Buck at center stage without having to make any commitments.

But to think of Buck Preston as all pouting brat is a mistake. The total woman was a good deal more than the public child. She, as others of her social station, was raised to be a woman of means who could manage means and hold it against all comers. A steel magnolia. She was brought up to the "high tempered" measure of her time and place, riding, hunting, and shooting. She was trained to help manage her husband's plantations – keep the accounts, oversee the overseers of slaves, plan the crops, order the raising of buildings and clearing of land, hire-fire-buy labor for an enterprise with far-flung fields, maybe a ship or rail spur, and a slave labor force that could reach into the hundreds. No different from Hood's own mother who managed the family's 225,000 acres while Dr. Hood played medical games in Philadelphia.

As important as the girl to Hood's state of mind were the comically unhappy circumstances surrounding what Hood took be their various engagements. Buck's friends marveled that she could tolerate such a man as a suitor and said so to her face. That hardened her sullen resistance to any suggestion of a formal break with Hood. But his repeated maimings in combat must have stunned Buck with his prospects as a husband, public hero or not. Each new crippling seemed to make Hood more determined to have her and that interfered with Buck's sport of teasing all the other boys. So Buck abused and insulted him with her mightiest effort, embarrassing at least some of her female onlookers.

Buck's antics had to be extremely trying and confusing for Hood, a man who was simply spoken, impatient, matured by war, accustomed to peremptory command, and convinced by Richmond courtiers that he was a reborn Arthurian knight. He had been tripped up by love when all he had aimed for was a dowry of social and political connections.

Hood's fumbling search of a wife ended when he took leave of Buck and marched his soldiers into Pennsylvania behind Lee. For Hood, this may have been a happy escape from social confusion into the certainties of war. It also was a journey into a lover's uncertainty. For Buck, it was merely relief, and happy return to dramatic pining for a distant lover, plus renewal of her multiple flirtations. Then came Gettysburg and Chickamauga.

* * *

Gettysburg and Chickamauga were the two great turning points in Hood's wartime career because the wounds he suffered in these battles flung him out of Lee's ensemble of command in the Army of Northern Virginia. First, Gettysburg. It was an accidental battle, made on the march to somewhere else. Scouting elements of gray and blue armies stumbled into each other outside the little Pennsylvania town and crossroads. Nearby units ran to support the scouts. Suddenly the two most powerful armies on the continent were in combat.

On July 1-3, 1863, Lee failed to deliver the crushing victory over the Army of the Potomac he had hoped to achieve with this, his second, invasion of the North. Lee wanted to teach "those people" of the North – safe, fat, lazy, complacent, as he saw them – to "feel the evils of war at their own door," as Davis put it, in order to persuade them to command their government to sue for peace and separation.[25] Lee wanted to throw the frighteners into Philadelphia, Harrisburg or New York City to draw on a Federal counterattack on ground of his choosing. That was Lee's typical and typically successful ploy – *Come attack me where I choose so I can beat you.* Lee put his army on the high ground of Seminary Ridge opposite the Federals on Cemetery Ridge and waited for the blue army to sweep across the intervening valley and attack. Lee wanted a repeat of the victorious slaughter at Fredericksburg, another Marye's Heights vision.

But the new commander of the Army of the Potomac, Major General George Gordon Meade, refused to attack. Meade, unexpectedly elevated from corps to army command just three days before, was unsure how responsive his new army would be to his orders. He believed he had no choice but to make a defensive fight. He stretched his 94,000 soldiers across the high ground of Cemetery Ridge south of Gettysburg and opposite Lee on Seminary Ridge. Then he waited for Lee to come to him with his 70,000. Meade intended to fight as though he were Lee.

Hood saw Lee's error in allowing the fight to grow at this place and in this way. On the second day of battle, he repeatedly urged a scrambling strike up onto undefended Little Round Top that would have allowed the Army of Northern Virginia to roll up the Union left flank and may have won the battle. But James Longstreet speaking for Lee repeatedly denied him permission to deviate from Lee's battle plan. Hood made his part of the fight as ordered. He led his division in the frontal assault on the Union left that Lee wanted and against a now well-defended Little Round Top. Hood was blown from his saddle and his troops thrown back. Even so, Hood's division – Rebel-yelling in their charge behind their berserker general – nearly broke the Union left.

Hot shrapnel ripped into Hood's left hand and ricocheted through his forearm, elbow, and biceps, ripping out muscle as it dragged into the wound infectious battle grime and shirt and jacket fibers. Amputation was not required. But, in those pre-antibiotic days, Hood's convalescence was long and miserable – no, not miserable, ghastly. Hood was crippled for life.

The following day, July 3, as Hood lay in great pain in a hospital tent, a frustrated Lee – "impatient of listening and tired of talking"[26] and believing he saw the chance for victory – ordered Pickett's Charge. Major General George Pickett led three divisions in a huge frontal assault into the solid center of the Union lines. Great battle is what Lee always craved and sought and what he made this day. Pickett's charge was blasted apart. The three days' battle lost. The Army of Northern Virginia withdrew southwards, leaving one-third of itself – 23,000 casualties – scattered ruins across the trampled wheat fields and orchards and in the makeshift hospitals of Gettysburg. With those lost to death and wounds died the offensive capacity of one of the greatest armies in American history. Desertions rose as soldiers abandoned Lee and trudged home. Lee submitted his resignation to Jefferson Davis. It was refused. What else could Davis do? Where would he find a better Lee?

Lee was not Lee at Gettysburg or perhaps he was more Lee because he was more alone in those three days without the best help of his great lieutenants. Stonewall Jackson was dead, killed two months before in a friendly fire incident in the battle of Chancellorsville, Virginia. Jeb Stuart was cowboying with his cavalry no one knew where around Gettysburg, depriving Lee of necessary intelligence on the Army of the Potomac. James Longstreet, Lee's "War Horse," had fallen into a depressed funk after Lee had shoved aside Longstreet's cool-headed advice to avoid a self-destructive battle at Gettysburg and, instead, speed down to strike Washington City. Yet what Lee did between those two murderous ridges outside a sleepy Pennsylvania town was true to the Confederate war plan and true to the Southern character at mid-century. What he did he could not avoid doing.

Hood returned to Richmond. The Adonis with his red badge of courage became the new lion of society, convalescing in the ease of female company, in Varina Davis's salon, in Mary Chesnut's parlor, telling his president thrilling tales of battle. There is no record what Hood thought of the arm hanging mangled and dead at his side. It is easy to imagine it a bitter loss to this man of passionate action. But this crippled Hood returned to Richmond no longer was the neophyte in social and political combat. He seems to have learned some things. His wound may have convinced him he deserved more than to be petted in the president's wife's salon. The cynicism he had applied to wife-hunting he now also applied to self-promotion.

With what historian Richard O'Connor aptly calls "ambition aforethought,"[27] Hood began to use the society that had scorned his social clumsiness to worm his way into the president's inner circle, into the power core of the Confederate government. The loss of an arm had put him in a position to do something great for himself. He could marry Buck and use his heroic crippling to begin an ascent in politics as rapidly as he had in the army. Or he could shuck his uniform for business, grow rich and fat and sit out the rest of the war. The trajectory of Hood's life, from his frontier origins and his family's social ambitions through heroic adventure toward the upper reaches of society, suggest that he would do one or the other. But Hood did not choose to do those rich and easy things and in that is a measure of a maturing character.

Buck's sullen indecision about marriage and a fresh fire invigorated in Hood by the president's admiration returned Hood to thinking of honest battle. His division, despairing over the Gettysburg disaster and anxious to shield beneath their general's combat luck, begged him to lead them into their next big fight. "They were destitute of almost everything, I might say, except pride, spirit, and forty rounds of ammunition to the man," Hood wrote in his memoir.[28] Those are brave words about brave men who deserved a brave leader. They also said, Responsibility.

That change was there now in Hood – not responsibility to Lee his mentor or to the newspapers acclaiming him a hero to the Cause. But acceptance of a moral responsibility to stand once more with comrades in a desperate moment, to make a self-less decision to fight when Hood honorably could have held back. All of Hood's makeup was there in this decision – the village bully boy, the cowboy cavalryman, the lionized hero, the battle-lover. So, too, was the stubborn Southern attitude of resistance to any challenge. Here was the first evidence of a more complete man.

When Hood's troops rode the trains through Petersburg, Virginia, toward the battle that would come at Chicka-mauga, Tennessee, on September 19-20, 1863, Hood put his favorite horse, "Jeff Davis," on the cars and went back to war with Longstreet's corps of the Army of Northern Virginia. He proposed to Buck once again, on the train platform. Her reply was equivocal or he chose to read it as positively as that. It was enough for now. He went happy to war.

Here, now, was the second great turning point in Hood's wartime career, the event that finally separated Hood from Lee. The young general – he was still young, at least by the calendar, just thirty-three – had been trained by the greatest fighting general of the South. He had learned enough from Richmond's biting scorn to maneuver and manipulate soci-ety. He had turned tables on that society by making a patron of their president. He had his eye set on a rich and alluring woman for his wife. And he had plenty of his trademark power to charge to victory. Hood was ready for a triumph. He was ready to become what Celebrity whispered he could become. He jumped his horse off the train and rode into combat.

"Jeff Davis" was shot from under Hood in the fighting before Chickamauga became a battle. The horse had been his good luck charm. Hood climbed onto another horse and was shot through the thigh. First reports to Richmond said he was dead, driving a public frenzy of despair. His leg had to be amputated just below the hip. He was carried to a nearby house to recover – his survival chances were less than fifty-fifty[29] – and eventually moved to Richmond, Adonis doubly crippled. More flutter of crinoline. The Davises lent him their personal carriage for transport around the city. Hood in public bore his second maiming as a hero must but it had to have been hard for a man of action to bear.

Hood had been glorious in the war's early years and, when he met Buck in spring of '63, he was fit, strong, and a Confederate hero. A half year later, after the crippling of an arm at Gettysburg and the loss of a leg at Chickamauga, Hood was still a national hero. But he no longer was a perfect golden boy. No longer a prime catch for a Southern belle with Buck's fortune and family. How does a man bed a "high tempered" young woman when he has only one useful arm and no leg but a knobby mass of scars? When he is in frequent pain and sometimes half-doped on laudanum? When, to remain the bold cavalier, he must have his aides strap him into the saddle, fitting his false leg into a stirrup for balance? When to defecate in an army latrine or to urinate in a chamber pot is a clumsy wretchedness?

Buck's parents, from the beginning distressed at the thought of her alliance with this dull social upstart, were aghast at the idea of her marrying a one-armed, one-legged man with what they considered the meagerest of post-war prospects. The Prestons had hedged their bet on the Confederacy by investing their money in New York and London. They hedged again on the Confederacy by bearing down on Buck, in league with her friends, to break her away from Hood. She was rebellious and might marry this human wreck to spite her parents. But, at Christmas 1863, when Hood proposed once more, she refused him outright. This time, he understood what she said.

Yet Hood persisted. He had to because he was Hood. In January, 1864, he ordered from Europe, to be brought by blockade runner through the Union navy's cordon of Southern ports, three cork legs and a diamond ring.

* * *

In February 1864, Hood was promoted to lieutenant general in reward for his services and his wounds and his horizon expanded immeasurably. In Hood's stubborn optimism, there seemed little in the Confederate world not open to him now. He could stump through London in gray uniform trimmed with gold, his Buckie on his arm, the Confederate States of America ambassador to the Court of St. James's, and show himself as a great character in the world's greatest city. Or he could go into the Confederate congress and look forward to a post-war, multi-titled life of aristocratic wealth and ease. Or, as he now had the rank to become an army commander, he might win a battle or two all by himself and run for president.

Hood tried to use these new prospects to win Buck from her parents. He failed. But, as the Confederacy's newest lieutenant general and the president's favorite about to be sent off to campaign with Joe Johnston against the vast blue power of William T. Sherman, Hood qualified once again as Buck's preferred type of lover – the absent sort – and she agreed, or let Hood think she agreed, to an engagement.

Contemporary witnesses say Buck's parents wept when the engagement was announced on February 12, 1864. It is easy enough to imagine their despair and frustration. They wept for Hood's lack of social standing, for his lack of an arm and a leg, for Buck's selfishness, for the family fortunes as-suredly to be thrown away by this cowboy, and for their own social embarrassment. Then Hood was gone, mercifully snapped away to fight off the blue invasion. Perhaps this war-mad young man might succeed in destroying the rest of himself in his next wild charge? One could hope. Hood gave Buck the diamond-studded silver star he wore in his hat and left for Dalton, Georgia, and the great and melancholy Army of Tennessee.

Down in Georgia, Buck now had a crippled war hero for whom to pine but here in Virginia, close by and available, she began to notice handsome Rawlins Lowndes, two-armed, two-legged, charging about with her uncle Wade Hampton's cavalry, and looking very much a hero-in-the-making.

* * *

Now Comes the Breaker of the Old Ways

For three years of battle, Northern resistance had proved barely adequate to contain Southern ambition for independence from the United States. So it seemed to people in the North. Eighteen-sixty-four opened looking to many in the North, including Lincoln, as the year of Southern victory by default.

Lee with his hotly mobile Army of Northern Virginia once again waited on the Rapidan River to ambush and humiliate the Army of the Potomac, the most powerful, best-equipped, best-trained, and most highly experienced of the armies in blue. James Longstreet was in East Tennessee, floundering for the moment but out there with his powerful corps from Lee's army in the very piece of real estate that so often had been fought over that this civil war almost could be called

"The War for Tennessee." P. G. T. Beauregard taunted the
Federal navy from Charleston, South Carolina, secession's
nest. General Edmund Kirby Smith sat serene and secure in
his "kingdom" in the vast Trans-Mississippi West. And, in
north Georgia, Joe Johnston, the general who worried hard
commanders like Grant and Sherman when they were un-
worried by Lee, had taken over the Army of Tennessee with
the mission to retake its home state, wreck Lincoln's re-elec-
tion chances in November, and win a negotiated peace.

From the perspective of Northern voters, 1864 looked like
yet another year of heartbreak and disappointment. Each
piece of territory won was lost and had to be won again, and
then it was threatened. Lee invaded the North and was
pushed back and invaded again. Gray armies were driven
out of Tennessee and swarmed in again and were driven out
again. Now Joe Johnston and the Army of Tennessee were
ready to march into the state once more. After three years of
fumbling failure – of lying politicians, incompetent generals,
worthless strategies – the people of the North were fed up
with war. Draft and race riots racked the North, along with
calls to throw out the dreary, bloody-handed, failed Lincoln
administration in the 1864 election. Or perhaps make it simple and stage a military coup that would order the war's end
with or without victory.

To read diaries and accounts of the Northern men and
women who lived through these hard times is to feel their

terrible sadness, so sunk in dread that hope seems nearly beyond reason. This civil war had become the Napoleonic horror predicted by Winfield Scott, the Ten Years War promised by Lee. Many in the North were convinced the South could not be whipped. Others wanted to forget the war and turn Northern energies into settling the West and making something grand out of the new power of industrialism. For some, the all-American making of money seemed a happier pursuit than killing white people for the sake of black people. After all, if the war were won, what would it do but return the ever-problematic South to the Union and then what – another seventy years of political bickering over regional power followed by another civil war?

Americans at mid-century had been an untried people unready for this colossal war. The war remade the people of the North. Coming into 1864, in all their fury and despair, they do not seem to have realized the changes in themselves, yet they were being changed. The war was driving them to become a better people than might have been expected of them after 350 years of narrow self-interest, greedy plunder of the New World, and a national economy made rich by slavery. Each day's death list in the newspapers brought new horror – more thousands slaughtered! a husband's love gone! a parent's hope snuffed out! – until people in the North, across the dreadful year of 1864, gradually came to decide that only victory would give meaning to so much loss. And so, too, they came, very slowly, to believe that victory would not bring peace if slavery survived. They had to kill the monster slavery and free the slaves to save themselves.

This idea gave the people of the North a new, grim, toughness of spirit. It gave them grit. The change was not immediately apparent when Grant set off on his spring campaign that year. But it became apparent as this hard year ground on. It was made certain on Election Day. This new spirit changed the character of the nation that survived the Civil War, making Americans a people who could survive the Great Depression, fight two world wars against increasingly more ghastly tyrannies, and stand their ground through fifty years' threat of nuclear annihilation in the Cold War. The Northern people and their new warlord, Ulysses S. Grant, were about to make 1864 a year so unlike the war years that had gone before that this was very nearly a different war.

* * *

Civil War photographs do not show the "Rufus" Grant his contemporaries knew, a man of twinkling eyes, round rosy cheeks, and a Will Rogers sense of humor, a shy man yet a secret glutton for the celebrity that came with three stars – the rank held by George Washington – and for the sudden promise of the Presidency, the customary reward for war-winning American generals. Grant was the most subtle military politician of the war and the least subtle strategist. Rufus would, he said in grisly style, hold the South as a man holds an orange and squeeze until it burst. The North too long had let itself be distracted by competing priorities – the lure of the West and the modernizing world – but Grant would make it concentrate on winning the war. He made his generals understand their task henceforth was to break enemy armies any way they could, at whatever cost, and that Sherman, the wild man from the West, would be their model army-breaker.

To shatter Southern power, Grant meant to destroy or pin down the gray armies and then burn out the South's capacity to feed and arm its armies. This was not a new strategic idea – Winfield Scott suggested it at the war's beginning, Lincoln tried to push it on his unwilling generals, even Henry Halleck proposed it[30] – but Grant made it his own in a unique way. He was a man burdened with a strange superstition he carried from boyhood, something unsettling for his enemies had they known of it. Grant could not go back up any road he had come down. He could not retreat. "One of my superstitions," he wrote in his *Memoirs*, "had always been when I started to go anywhere or to do anything, not to turn back, or stop until the thing intended was accomplished."[31] And he so hated war that he chose to make it with overwhelming power and speed in order to end it quickly. His war plan was relentless attack on all combat fronts. Grant meeting with Sherman en route to Washington City to assume his new rank – on March 9, 1864 – as lieutenant general and general-in-chief of all Federal armies drew five blue arrows on his war map. Those were his fingers crushing the Confederate fruit. He kept for himself the arrow pointing at Lee and the Army of Northern Virginia. He gave the second arrow – pointing at Joe Johnston and the Army of Tennessee – to Sherman. He apportioned the rest among his other commanders. Go, he said to his generals, *and smash them.*

Grant had no war plan beyond those five blue arrows. He knew he had to be winning the war before the November elections or the war would be lost at the ballot box.

* * *

The South was not prepared for Grant's new kind of war. The stubborn willingness of barefoot men in tattered gray to keep up the fight for secession over three long years had astonished and appalled the people of the North and gave Confederate political leadership its most powerful tool in winning Northern hearts and minds for separation. But the Southern war plan – unchanged from the war's first days and grown from a slave-holding temper, a misreading of European politics, over-confidence in the warrior spirit, and the romance of a revolutionary age – was about to come up hard against a new kind of Northern strategist and commander.

Confederate political and military leadership had changed little since 1861. An unchanged leadership offered no new strategic thinking for 1864. Davis had swapped his generals among assignments to punish combat failure and to skewer political opponents. But most of the men who had begun the war in senior commands remained in senior command in the war's last year. Their ideas were used up. They were exhausted men. Their dyspeptic and irritable president considered himself a master strategist and what point their competing with him? At the beginning of it all, Davis and Lee both had said the war could run ten years and so apparently it must.

The Confederacy was very slow to recognize in Grant the North's changed strategic approach and could not – would not – find an original response. In a war started to resist change, in a society with the habit of stonewalling any challenge, and a Confederacy fighting for an ideal – self-determination – that all reasonable people must approve, why change strategy or leaders?

Yet something had to be done. The South's native resources were being used up. Even new, fast blockade-runners could not haul past the Union fleet enough European goods to sustain the war. The black market in cotton – selling into Mexico and across the combat line to New York speculators – brought in too little cash.[32] The Confederacy was running out of money. European banks would lend no more. Federal armies wherever they marched were burning out the South's economic base – firing crops and towns, tearing up railroads. The country was racked by tax and bread riots. Worse, the South was running out of white men to put on the firing line.

The Confederate dream had been ravaged and driven into international isolation and the Southern people had seen their new nation transformed into a militarized and vigilante state. To doubt the wisdom of the war, the certainty of victory, the brilliance of a Confederate future or ever to have said an unkind word about slavery was un-Confederate and disloyal, bringing to the door the hooded vigilante with torch, pistol, and rope. Closet Unionists were rooted out. Indifferentists among the old, poor, and weak were bullied and beaten. Accused "Lincolnites" had their hearts cut out and their property divided among the neighbors who had denounced them. Vigilantes hanged slaves who cheered the arrival of Federal troops. "We seceded to rid ourselves of the rule of the majority," said Jefferson Davis.[33] But what Southerners got was rule by what Mark Twain called "the aggressive and pitiless minority." The North committed its own outrages against liberty but nothing like this.

Even where enemy armies had not penetrated, the war was killing the South, starving its white and black families, sickening its children, stripping its fields and shops to feed and supply the gray armies. The war cost the North 250 lives and a stupendous two and one-half million dollars each day. But the North was growing richer as its economy modernized and its population outgrew its war losses. The undivided United States had the world's largest economy after Great Britain's and the rump United States could afford this war. And perhaps it could afford all the other wars it chose to risk at the same time – with the Plains Indians, with Britain over recognition of the Confederacy, with France over Mexico, and a naval fight with Japan. The South could not equal that growing economic and military power.

But the South still had that fiercely driving Confederate soldier. Despite lost battles, dwindling resources, and the unexpected cutting away of much international support by Lincoln's Emancipation Proclamation of January 1, 1863 – which converted this into a war to end slavery – the man in gray with a gun still dominated Northern morale. He was determined to cast his vote for separation in the November election. Lincoln and Grant thought that man in gray would win the election if he could threaten to stretch out the war just one more year. Do that and the weary North would vote for a President who promised a negotiated separation and quick peace.

That prospect may not have been evident to the desperate Southern woman on a ruined farm, her husband gone away to the army, hungry children at her knees, but it was evident to Northern leaders. Could gray soldiers hold out long enough to drive demoralized Northerners to cry, "Peace!" before the South used up itself in 1864?

[Part II]

The New Civil War of 1864

All that has gone before is mere Skirmishing – The War now begins...

– Sherman in a letter to his wife[34]

WHEN THE SPRING CAMPAIGNS OPENED in May of 1864, neither side had the arithmetic to win the war. Lieutenant General Ulysses S. Grant, new-made commander of all United States land forces, with twenty-one army corps and 533,000 fighting men at his command across the continent,[35] could not bring enough weight to bear to crush the Confederacy outright. As Grant's forces carved away pieces of the South, the smaller Confederate armies were left with a more defendable frontier and greater capacity for quick mutual support. This allowed them to so raise the cost to Federal armies of holding Southern territory that nearly half of Grant's available combat troops were marching sentry duty beside rail and telegraph lines and supply warehouses in enemy country.[36] The Confederacy's over 200,000 troops, operating in friendly territory and largely free of that kind of responsibility, could be enough to hold off whatever maneuver forces Grant could spare to send against them. A gaudy victory or two might even draw back to the colors the 100,000 Confederate deserters, many of them men pulled away to their farms by their families' hunger, and how would that shift the war's direction?[37]

But size is not power in an army. For armies north and south in 1864, most of the best men and officers, those with courage, drive, and zeal for the cause who had run early to join the colors, were gone. They were dead, wounded, invalided or mustered out, simply vanished in battle or disappeared into the great and quiet West. Their kind in the remaining manpower pool was nearly used up. Their absence changed the character of the armies making them workmanlike things without bravado. Too many replacements on both sides were the dredgings of the press gangs – unwilling, unpatriotic, too young, too old, too weak. They and their lack of experience, training, and will made the armies difficult to handle, slow to respond, unimaginative in spotting combat opportunities and slow to grasp them.

These armies could be trained into stand-up sluggers but they no longer were capable of the elegant surprise punch. The war had gone on too long for the good of the armies.

As winter melted into muddy spring, the armies blue and gray burnished weapons and issued shoes and began to look up the roads leading toward the new campaigning season. Governments on both sides of the Mason-Dixon Line prepared to push their armies toward Northern Election Day. The desperate hour of success or failure had arrived. Into this wild moment, Jefferson Davis shoved his newest lieutenant general and nearly the South's last hope, John Bell Hood. Davis expected Hood to provide the bold stroke that would startle the planet and rouse to the South's salvation the somnolent European powers and the peace party in the North. *Hood is the new Jackson!* cried the newspapers. *He will win the war!* But Hood had no army to command and he had to get one.

Hood, fresh from the pettings of the president's wife's salon, from an overlong dalliance in South Carolina with his Buckie, robust despite his savage injuries, and riding horseback despite the lack of an arm and a leg, arrived at the headquarters of the Army of Tennessee at Dalton, Georgia, in early February expecting a hero's welcome. What he found were general officers morose and suspicious of one another. An army still recovering from defeat by Grant at Chattanooga, Tennessee, and doubtful of its leadership. And an army commander – Joseph E. Johnston – devoid of Lee-like dynamism and who seemed ready to retreat before his campaign to retake Tennessee had even begun. Or that is how Hood reported the scene in his autobiography.

The coming fight in the West, over Tennessee, would start here in Georgia and be made by two champions – Sherman and Johnston – with the impatient Hood waiting for his cue to greatness. Sherman, commander of all Federal forces in the West, was brilliant and bitter, unstable, an anti-democrat, and a racist. He made war because he despised secessionists for seeking to overthrow duly appointed authority. Yet late in the war he proposed seizing the great Southern plantations for breaking up and parceling out to each freed slave forty acres and a mule.

Contemporaries describe Sherman as a frenetic man of ideas yet he was a surprisingly conventional soldier. He had been horrified to watch Grant cut his army loose from traditional dependence on supply lines to make a great flank march down the Mississippi River to capture Vicksburg in 1863. Then Sherman modeled his own March to the Sea across Georgia on Grant's idea, adding his trademark Thor's hammer approach.

Joe Johnston, commander of the Army of Tennessee, was a well-tailored dandy, a sharp but not clever politician, a tough, wily, and experienced but very conventional commander. As a brigadier general in the old U.S. Army, he was the highest ranking officer to join the Confederate States Army. He hated his president and despaired of the direction of Confederate military strategy. Sherman and Grant knew and feared Johnston. Their judgment of him must be accepted, though looking at Johnston's war record from this distance makes it hard to understand.

Unlike Hood, whose cynical social-climbing was ambushed by love, Johnston was by nature a sentimentalist and romantic. As a young officer, he loved to tease and be teased by pretty Indian girls under an Alabama moon. When he found a woman to marry, he loved her with teenage devotion and trusted no one but her to know his full heart and mind. That was a trust he did not extend even in limited degree to his president.

Success or failure for Johnston and Sherman depended on the support and freedom of action granted each by his national command authority. Sherman had his President's whole-hearted support. Johnston had his president's contempt. He also had, like a grim shadow at his back, the president's "pet and minion," Hood, watching and reporting his every action.

From the war's beginning, Johnston and Davis had been like two dogs latched onto a bone too small for either but each unwilling to let the other have it. Johnston was of that great number of Americans who believes in his rights and that he must have them, period. Davis was one of that breed of men who considers every slight a grave insult and bears grudges into eternity. Their enmity began when they were cadets together at West Point. Legend has it rooted in a fist-fight over a tavern keeper's daughter. That story is too good not to be true, as the French say. Whatever the first cause, at the war's beginning the president and his general were delighted to renew their old quarrel in an absurd running argument over Johnston's precedence of rank based on his Old Army grade. That became the lightning rod for their political competition and personal enmity across the entire war. Johnston carried the feud into the post-war years.

But the key to their public combat was the debate over national military strategy. In a raucous and individualistic age, in a people's war, in a self-proclaimed revolutionary nation, no debate on military strategy could avoid becoming savage political debate. Johnston drew around himself such an anti-Davis faction that, by 1864, he and that conniving super-secessionist, Vice President Alexander H. Stephens, had become the spearheads of domestic opposition to Davis.

Davis was chosen for his office because the leading men of the South considered him the best combination politician, military man, and diehard for the Cause among them. Arthritic and one-eyed but true to his Southern character, Davis would have preferred to be a corps or army commander for the pleasure of leading wild charges against the hated enemy. He considered himself a military genius. He despised Johnston for having had what Sherman called "the most exalted reputation with our old army as a strategist"[38] and for the arrogance of Johnston's in-your-face strategic arguments. Davis stood with Lee for a concentration of war effort in the East, the theater of the two warring capitals and of the two most powerful opposing armies. Johnston's cabal demanded a Western strategy where they believed the war would be won by gray armies ranging rapidly across the continent, laughing at Northern incapacity to catch them, and falling in surprise assaults on blue centers of gravity to crush Federal military power and drain Northern popular will to continue the war.

Richmond demanded hotly aggressive warlords everywhere to stall what it knew would be a desperate, election year push by Federal forces. The defense-minded Johnston looked a bad fit with that demand, and not simply in Davis's view. Johnston seemed to Richmond to behave too much like a military aristocrat whose high reputation carried over from the Old Army gave him the freedom to avoid bloody battle and, instead, seek the elegant maneuver to win without fighting. To the gimlet-eyed decision-makers in Richmond, Johnston was an accountant of war who so carefully measured cost and benefit that his fighting style became one of always backing up to find better ground and a better moment to fight and too often never finding ground or moment. He was the coiled snake that would not strike.

Looking at his war record is to understand that Johnston tried to operate in that Clausewitzian turning point when a long defense shifts to counterattack and victory. His fighting style was not much different from Lee's, who invited attack so that he could fight from the advantage of the defensive. But Johnston loved maneuver while Lee loved to fight, so the turning point came less readily to Johnston – or to his perception – than to Lee. Yet Lee admired him and, in 1865, demanded of the Confederate government that Johnston finish the war in honorable command of an army.[39]

Richmond knew that Atlanta was Sherman's objective and expected the Army of Tennessee to make a hundred mile defense in depth out of Tennessee and across northern Georgia to the city. Richmond also expected that, somewhere along those hundred miles, the gray army would counterattack to inflict a decisive defeat on Sherman. But would the too-careful Johnston find his turning point?

For an officer who may have held more field commands than any other in the Civil War, Johnston fought few full-scale battles – just Seven Pines, Virginia, in 1862, Kennesaw Mountain, Georgia in 1864, and Bentonville, North Carolina, in 1865. He proposed abandoning the Peninsula to Union commander George B. McClellan in 1862 and only the sudden arrival of the ironclad fighting ship *CSS Virginia* and some earthworks thrown up by Confederate sailors saved Richmond from abandonment and capture by McClellan in the war's second year. Johnston refused to relieve John C. Pemberton besieged in Vicksburg, Mississippi, by Grant in 1863 because it was impractical and a waste of casualties – that accountant's assessment – and Vicksburg was lost to the

South and the Mississippi River with it. He seemed to many of his contemporaries as a Southern man without the requisite hot blood. When the 1864 campaign season opened, Johnston had seen no combat since Seven Pines – where he was severely wounded and replaced in army command by Lee. He had no active field service since Vicksburg.

For all of these reasons, Johnston was not Richmond's first choice to command the South's second great army. Yet his national command authority gave him the job and for three good reasons. First, the Confederacy had run out of generals qualified for army command who were not combat failures, politically poisonous to Davis or unwilling to take the job. The Confederacy, in contrast to the Union, did a poor job of training up replacement generals, Hood's inadequate seasoning a good example. Lee refused the command because he doubted the Army of Tennessee would accept him. Second, Johnston's political support – from the vice president and many in congress – had to be appeased. Third, the strategic situation in the West was so bad that, whether Johnston whipped or was whipped, Davis would have a personal victory. One more of Johnston's trademark fighting retreats without victorious battle would make Johnston's political suicide and disrupt the anti-Davis faction for good.

Johnston understood all of this but also saw himself and Lee – as Lee also saw them both – as the last great commanders standing for the Confederacy. There were no more armies to be called out of the Southern population because there were no more white men to recruit. Families at home were starving to keep the last two large field forces – the Armies of Tennessee and Northern Virginia – on the battle line. Johnston could not squander a single soldier's life or artillery shell or pound of gunpowder, flour or axle grease. Every bit and piece of his army had to be maintained and made to strike the enemy with maximum efficiency and maximum impact. Johnston knew Richmond expected him to create a Sherman-smashing battle – as Richmond expected Lee to smash Grant – and to send the shattered blue wreckage weeping into Northern polling places on Election Day. But to do that Johnston had to change his combat style – he had to be more like Lee.

Jefferson Davis expected Hood to make a Lee out of Johnston. Davis seemed to expect that Hood, by example of his combat fire and loyalty to the president, would squelch the tiresome officer factionalism disrupting smooth command leadership in the Army of Tennessee and inoculate the army and its commander with the fierce drive of the Army of Northern Virginia. It was a good idea and the only acceptable option – acceptable to Davis – available. But it was the triumph of hope over experience in Davis's dealings with Johnston.

* * *

DECISION FOR A GENERAL'S COUP

Johnston had no delusions about the purpose of Hood's assignment to the army but may not have considered Davis was grooming this freshly-made lieutenant general to replace him. Johnston was tough and perceptive and operated behind a veil of good cheer, good manners, and gentlemanly reserve, making him a hard man for his contemporaries to read. He remains difficult to read for historians. He received Hood warmly and not as the rival Hood perceived himself to be. He gave Hood his junior corps, with 17,000 men. He flattered the younger man by repeatedly asking his advice in war conferences, though it must have been hard for Johnston, so proud and arrogant, to endure hearing advice from this tattletale and inferior.

For his part, Hood had to feel himself very near the apex of a soldier's dream. He had come from the hothouse of Richmond's adulation and the victory of achieving an engagement with Buck to be here, at the army commander's planning table, preparing to launch a great army against an invading horde. He was being treated with the confidence and deference he expected. He appears to have believed he had conned Johnston and that Johnston genuinely admired him. Hood had been ambushed by love and now he was about to be ambushed by Joe Johnston.

Hood gave Johnston Richmond's plan for reconquering Middle Tennessee. The plan called for Johnston's army to drive north to be reinforced by Lieutenant General Leonidas Polk's army from Louisiana and Longstreet's corps from Virginia. These forces combined would crush and scatter Sherman's armies and retake Tennessee. It was a good plan. Johnston was unenthusiastic. He was suspicious of any plan dependent on promises of coordinated efforts by others, especially when his army would march first into the teeth of the blue juggernaut. After what had happened to General Braxton Bragg, Johnston's predecessor in command of this army, when a lost battle meant a humiliating cashiering, Johnston was suspicious of the political risk of battlefield failure. He was suspicious of the motive behind any order he received from Davis.

Hood was startled by and suspicious of Johnston's suspicions. He could not understand why Johnston did not do as Lee would do when given the opportunity to fight – gather up all this wealth of men and weapons and attack. Hood, continuing to receive instructions from Davis and Davis's military advisor Bragg, tried to goad Johnston to action and reported back to Davis on Johnston's hesitations.

Johnston was a romantic but he was not romantic about the Confederate cause and that is what Hood failed to understand. Johnston, as Lee, was a man of the "old confederacy of these united states" who believed he owed loyalty first to his family and then to his state and a good deal later to a loose central government empowered to provide the nation's external defense and not much more. He opposed slavery and had opposed secession. He did his duty in the Confederate war but there was no revolutionary fervor in him. He would have managed his relations with his president better had he shown at least a theatrical fervor. Or had he learned to be as able a manipulator of his president and the Confederate congress as Lee. Hood came to see Johnston as a plodding dandy who could not be moved to fight.

Johnston's long defense from Dalton to Atlanta holding back Sherman was, for Hood, two months of astonishment and frustration. Of digging and retreating before Sherman's equally dull but relentless advance. Of never coming to grips with the terrible enemy, of no effort to bash out his brains and whoop the victory cheer. And of the deaths of too many of Hood's friends. "What followed at Resaca?" Hood later wrote in his memoir, his exasperation still evident. "Retreat. New Hope Church? Retreat. Cassville? Retreat. Kennesaw Mountain? Retreat." Johnston "invariably throws up entrenchments, fortifies his line, and there remains in deliberation upon the best means to defeat the enemy without risking a general engagement, when, suddenly, he finds himself outflanked, and issues the usual order for retreat."[40]

After the grisly sacrifices Hood had made for the Cause and feeling the eyes of Reputation and of the woman he loved on his every action, Hood thought Johnston's fallback strategy intolerable and not the way any Southern army should operate. But Hood was not the army commander. He could not win this campaign until he had command. When would Davis give him the army? Or would the president delay so long that Hood would sink into ignominy alongside Johnston for having retreated until the army splashed into the Gulf of Mexico? Hood sank into a depression.

In his self-absorption, frustration, and inexperience managing an army corps, Hood repeatedly failed Johnston's battle plans at critical moments – at Cassville Road and Adairsville, in particular. He contributed to the failure of other assaults that Johnston put in motion. Not all Johnston's fumbles can be blamed on Hood but more of them than should be the share of any one corps commander. They show that, without the good management provided by Lee but not by Johnston, Hood could not make himself fully effective. A corps commander needs more than Hood's self-confidence and good press to be a success. He needs a foxy drive supported by his subordinates and fellow corps commanders and leveraged by his army commander. Hood, by the subversive nature of his mission to this army, had denied himself all those supports. Perhaps that is where Johnston wanted Hood to be.

Despairing, harassed by his president, driven by the imp of ambition, Hood began preparations to stage a coup against his commanding officer. His correspondence with Davis and Buck make clear that, even before he left Richmond for Georgia, Hood expected to take the command and that he believed Davis wanted him to have it. Now he felt it as much his duty as the president's to arrange for the moment when Johnston could be fired and Hood promoted. Hood did not consider this as disloyalty to a commander in the face of the enemy but as necessary and patriotic. Nor was his kind of scheming unusual in Civil War armies on either side of the battle line, composed as they often were of self-proclaimed American individualists whose ambition disguised as patriotism could be set free in the anarchy of wartime.

I am, Hood wrote Davis in letter after letter unsophisticated and self-promoting, *a hot-tempered combat leader and "an earnest friend to the President.'* How Davis read these letters is uncertain. Davis was too astute to be taken in by his young general. Yet Hood was out there living the dream of the wild, young Louisiana Rifleman still inside Davis.

Hood's correspondence with Davis remains a large part of the partisan debate that still clusters about Hood. Did he conspire to steal the command or did he merely shake the tree to let fall the ripened fruit? Was he so distracted by his Buckie or his depression as to be unaware of the likely effect of his correspondence? Was he set up by the anti-Davis/pro-Johnston crowd, as some contemporaries thought, to take the blame for the inevitable loss of Atlanta? Or were his fawning letters to his Machiavellian president too good an opportunity for Davis not to exploit?

There is a simple way to answer these questions and it lies in an older mystery. Did Richard III seal up in the Tower of London and kill the two little princes who were his rivals for the English crown or did he not? It was to his advantage to kill them and to his disadvantage to leave them alive. Conclusion, he killed them. Hood saw it to his advantage to destroy his commanding officer and to his disadvantage – in multiple ways – to leave him in place, so Hood destroyed him.

* * *

Johnston got the order sweeping him from command before midnight July 17, 1864. How startling strange it must have been to Johnston to discover all his sly efforts wasted – Hood wriggled out of his grip to become his Iscariot, Davis winner in this latest round of their long feud, and the tactical marvel of his fallback campaign to Atlanta scorned as failure. All because Richmond and the people of the South had expected him to do what a Southern general must do – attack – and he had not. He had tried to win the war, instead.

Johnston had dodged and twisted around the thrusts of a vast invading power, delaying Sherman and his horde to run out the Northern election calendar and to buy time for the Confederate government to come up with a fresh strategy to beat the new kind of war foisted on the South by Grant. But no new ideas had come out of Richmond. The seventy-four days of Johnston's fallback campaign were wasted. Richmond was exhausted of new thinking, certain the obvious rightness of its cause must bring in European help, convinced the hell-raising power of shoeless, hungry, depleted gray soldiers would continue to beat blue armies, determined to stay the course with a strategy and with military and political leaders chosen long before Grant's new war. That is why Richmond fired Johnston, the South's best general at fighting a long defense, and gave his army to Hood, a general all knew would attack because attack was what Hood did and the Southern people expected.

If Johnston was surprised when the ax fell, he was not surprised it was falling. He had prepared for this moment to save his reputation and the record of his fallback campaign. *Hood, he would tell the world, was Mars sent me by the president, so how could all the blame for the campaign's failure be mine?* That sly maneuver off-balanced Johnston's political enemies and helped taint Hood's reputation to the present day.

As for Hood, he was surprised and frightened at what he had wrought and, a few hours after midnight, changed his mind about what he wanted.

* * *

By 1864, the war had become about capturing Richmond in the East and making a fighting road race in the West to get to Richmond. Not that commanders blue or gray cared about the city. But the Confederate capital had become the flash point for the grand, cataclysmic battle the weary North and desperate South craved to end the war. Each of the two Western armies – the Confederate Army of Tennessee and Sherman's Western "army group" – had to get to Richmond to join their Eastern armies to mass sufficient power to win the war. The secondary goal for each was to prevent the other Western army from getting there first.

To win the war, Grant in the Eastern theater had to end the amazing offensive power of Lee's Army of Northern Virginia by destroying it or nailing it in place. He could not allow it to support or join forces with the Army of Tennessee. He expected to eat away and ruin Lee's army in continuous combat or drive it to starvation and capitulation by denying it the resources needed to continue the fight. But Grant was not sure he had soldiers enough of sufficient quality to do the job.

Through the first months of the new year, Grant, Sherman in the West, and George Gordon Meade commanding the Army of the Potomac in the East stood at their campfires grinding their cigars in their teeth and watching their armies legally desert them. The men who had volunteered for three years' duty in 1861 were free to go home and they went home. Who could expect more? These were brave men who deserved their peace. Let others who had not yet put on their nation's uniform join the ranks to carry on the task.

The Veteran Volunteer Act, with its furloughs and four hundred dollar bounties for reenlistment, hoped to lure back these veterans. But there was no way for Grant, Sherman or Meade – or Lee or Johnston – to know how many men would return to fight under the striped flag. Confederate troops were amused, intrigued, and envious to watch so much of their enemy simply disappear. Men in gray were in for the duration. Of course, Lincoln could order up replacement regiments for Grant but those would be unwilling conscripts – "handcuffed volunteers" – and career bounty men. Armies made up of too many of these begrudging kinds could not frighten the tough and supple troops of Lee and Johnston, nor could Grant move and fight them as well as he could volunteers. Grant needed his veterans.

So Grant waited, seemingly impassive, this man who so compressed and internalized his anxieties that on the running fight to Appomattox in April 1865 he had days of pounding headache relieved instantly the moment he read Lee's surrender offer. Jitterbug Sherman paced and fretted in the West. Meade in the East threw down his big hat and cursed. Grant chose midnight on May 3 to begin the war of 1864 and waited for reports of the numbers returned to duty to calculate if he had armies enough to make his fights down those five blue arrows of invasion he had sketched on a map of the South.

Sherman was in the toughest position. He could not put his Western army group into motion against Joe Johnston until he made a head count of the last returning veterans on May 1. Even then half of whatever army he could assemble was entitled to go home that October.[41] Managing personnel in Sherman's army was like clerking at a railway station – get them in, fight them, send them home, find another batch, do it again. And hope to win Sherman's part of the war before he ran out of veterans to season the green recruits.

Meade's Army of the Potomac, the North's key fighting element because it opposed Lee and because it was Grant's field headquarters, was in little better shape. It, too, was made up largely of three-year volunteers, exhausted men who believed, quite reasonably, that the stay-at-homes should be made to fill their places in the ranks. Whether or not the stay-at-homes could be dragged away from the enriching excitements of the new industrial age or intercepted en route to Western adventure or pulled away from wives, children, and war-flourishing farmsteads or workshops was another matter.

But, by mid-April 1864, 136,000 veterans had reenlisted or, in their language, "veteranized" themselves for three more years of fighting. Most signed up to fight with Sherman, a commentary on "Uncle Billy" and how the rank-and-file saw the direction of the war in the West. Far fewer chose to return to the Army of the Potomac. Meade had to find another 30,000 recruits to fill out his ranks, and that at a time when Northern despair meant only half as many recruits were drawn into the military as the number of troops the armies were discharging. Nevertheless, about half of Meade's veterans re-enlisted. These men were granted furloughs home as their reward.

The furlough was a man's chance to live again among wife and children, parents, Old Grandpap who had stood in the British and Indian fire in 1812. A chance to be human for a span of time, to measure where the world was going. To dream of a future beyond the next half-cooked meal, the next bloody trench line, the next breathless run to a fight. The chance to be himself. In that moment of self-ness, men discovered or renewed or simply accepted in themselves a personal need to carry on the war to remake their country. A new moral grit had come into the soldiers as it was coming into the character of the people of the North and Grant had his armies.

* * *

After midnight on May 3-4, 1864, Grant opened the major operational phase of the North's new strategy to win the war along his five blue arrows. He ordered Meade's Army of the Potomac to move out to destroy or immobilize the Army of Northern Virginia or to separate it from its covering of Richmond so that Grant could take the Confederate capital.

The Army of the Potomac descended into Virginia in a series of great flanking movements. Grant always strove to limit bloodshed by advancing as "rapidly as possible to save hard fighting."[42] But Lee had the advantage of interior lines and geography and of hotly spirited gray troops. He dodged each of Grant's swinging blows and chopped down Federal soldiers to drive up the death toll in Northern newspapers. Grant failed to catch Lee. Lee failed to divert Grant from Richmond. They brought upon themselves the siege at Richmond/Petersburg that both dreaded.

But Grant had chewed another Gettysburg out of Lee's strength. Grant began his Potomac-to-Richmond campaign with 118,000 men to Lee's 64,000.[43] Grant killed or wounded 24,000 of Lee's troops, cutting away one-third of Lee's refreshed combat power.[44] The Army of the Potomac took fearsome losses, as well, but those were replaceable from the much larger Northern manpower pool. The South had to strain to provide Lee a few new men for each company and regiment Grant blew away.

Grant determined to keep Lee's remaining 50,000 veterans and replacements so tightly bottled up in Richmond and Petersburg as to prevent their reinforcing other Southern armies while Grant's "spare army" led by his terrible acolyte Sherman performed the greatest flanking action of the war scourging the cities, farms, and railroads of Georgia to starve Lee as Sherman made his way to join Grant for the last cataclysmic battle.

The war had worn away the quality in armies on both sides of the combat line. Conducting a siege was as much as

Grant could hope to get from the Army of the Potomac of 1864. Accepting siege was as much as Lee could manage. But Grant had squeezed out of the war the South's premier field force and that was a huge achievement. If his Virginia campaigns did not produce the war-winning battle of annihilation craved by the desperate people of the North, Lee bottled up in Richmond was success enough to allow Grant's larger plan to move ahead elsewhere.

Grant's genius was to consider a battle won or lost as nothing more than introduction to the next battle and that to the next. Individual combats were tools to be exploited. No battle was lost or won without being made part of the grand flow of his plan toward victory. But Northern voters saw something else. For them, no siege of starving soldiers around a city filled with starving women and children, even if intended to support some mysterious continental machination, could equal the sweet satisfying simplicity of a white flag on Lee's sword. "Who shall revive the withered hopes that bloomed at the beginning of General Grant's campaign?" cried the New York *World*.[45]

Grant's war plan seemed to be failing everywhere. Northern voters despaired to watch Lee evade Grant in the East and Johnston evade Sherman in the West. Could those hot and quick gray armies ever really be caged? Federal campaigns in the Shenandoah Valley and by the Army of the James toward Petersburg had failed. Major General Nathaniel P. Banks had forgotten to take Mobile, Alabama, and wandered up the Red River to capture Texas cotton for Northern mill interests, and incidentally to startle the French in their conquest of Mexico. Fast, new Confederate steamships skipped through the tighter Union blockade, hauling out cotton and hauling in European war supplies. And who really believed Robert E. Lee could be kept in any trap? Tomorrow or the day after, he would slip out of Richmond and past Grant as easily as he had Grant's predecessors and materialize parading down Pennsylvania Avenue in the nation's capital with flapping flags and a victory cheer. Or perhaps, good God, on Broadway, in pro-secession New York City with its race hate, draft riots, and dislike of a war that turned too much of the nation's focus away from Wall Street.

In fact, the ever-aggressive Lee was living up to Northern expectations. He proposed to Davis his third great raid on the North. It would be an invasion with more dramatic flourish than any hope of military achievement. But it would shiver the political landscape of the North before Election Day. Lee proposed sending troops to free Confederate prisoners of war at Point Lookout, Maryland, arm them, take the fort's artillery, and march on Washington City.[46] If half-starved P.O.W.s could not make much battle, they and their red flags would make a quick, cheap, and startling reminder of the South's spoiler power. That could be victory enough, considering the despair into which many Northern voters had sunk at Grant's failure to win the war quickly.

Grant was about to dis-elect Lincoln. The Radical Republicans had made Lincoln President in 1860. Grant's apparent failure persuaded them of the need to sweep out Lincoln, Grant, and all the other hacks who lacked the true abolitionist and South-hating spirit and replace them with heroes with vengeful murder in their hearts. The Radicals deserted Lincoln for John C. Fremont, a man insufficiently bloody-minded but a stalwart for a Constitutional amendment to banish slavery, install a civil rights law, apply Congressional reconstruction to the South, and distribute to soldiers confiscated Rebel land. Fremont was the man to start the work of putting the war down the right track.

But the Radicals' desertion to Fremont divided pro-union strength, threatening to throw the election to the independence-for-peace Democrats and their candidate, George B. McClellan, the general Lincoln had cashiered for failing to prosecute the war with speed and effectiveness.

Lincoln, seeing that he was too sweet for the Radicals and too sour for the Democrats, came to the dismal conclusion he would lose the election and the Confederacy would be set free by the President and Congress that followed him. In late August, Lincoln wrote his famous "secret letter" of despair confessing he expected to lose the election and the country. He sealed the letter to be opened after Election Day.

Yet the Confederate strategic position by late summer of 1864 stood on a razor's edge and Grant and Sherman knew it. So did Lee and Johnston. So did Lincoln, though he could not grasp the thing that would tip the Confederacy into giving up the war. Lee had wrecked the Army of Northern Virginia at Gettysburg and now he was bottled up in Richmond by Grant. Edmund Kirby Smith's army was stranded on the far side of the Union-controlled Mississippi River. The Army of Tennessee was the South's last major field force still free to maneuver and Sherman was about to bottle it up in Atlanta. But what next? What more? How to tip the Confederacy off the razor's edge?

The Republican Party depleted of the Radicals re-nominated Lincoln, unhappily and grudgingly, because it had no one else remotely capable of carrying on the war against slavery. And because Lincoln could bring in the soldier vote. After a party of principle's first victory at the polls, the party's continuing to win becomes more important than principle. If the soldiers would reelect Lincoln, the Republicans could stay in power. Lincoln's a bum, but he's our bum, so let him win this election for us and maybe win the war. Time enough afterward for the reckoning when all Republicans can enjoy watching the Radicals impeach the Great Ape for his lack of abolitionist purity and his multiple failures of leadership and character.

Now, nearly at summer's end, with Grant having failed to beat Lee in Virginia and win the election for Lincoln, Republican hopes shifted to Sherman in Georgia facing the Army of Tennessee.

* * *

On May 7, 1864, a few days after Grant began his pursuit of Lee to Richmond, Sherman marched out of Nashville, Tennessee, with 120,000 men in his Western army group – the Federal armies of the Tennessee, the Ohio, and the Cumberland – for the 138 mile descent into Georgia. Grant had begun the new war in the East. Now Sherman began the new war in the West. He had made sure each of his reenlisted veterans – the hard core of his power – had good new shoes and uniforms, burnished rifles, and plenty of bullets in their pockets. Sherman was determined the men whose grit had brought them back to the fight had what they needed to destroy those who had brought on this awful war.

Grant had given Sherman three objectives. First, prevent the Confederate Army of Tennessee from reinforcing Lee against Grant while Grant kept Lee away from Sherman so Sherman could "knock Joe Johnston."[47] Second, take Atlanta, gateway to the rich granaries and war factories that supported Lee at Richmond. Third, "strike for salt water" along any route opportunity might offer, wrecking everything in his path as he marched to destroy the South's capacity to continue the war. Sherman was to be to Grant what the strategic bombing forces were to British and American strategy in World War II – he was to destroy Southern centers of gravity to drive to collapse the Confederate field forces.

What Grant envisioned for Sherman was a gigantic but conventional raid, amplified by Nathaniel Banks pushing east from Mobile to meet Sherman at Atlanta for a massive joint thrust toward Savannah or the Gulf or any other place that seemed profitable to assault. But Sherman's striking power would dwindle as he garrisoned troops in his wake to protect his single, 138 mile rail line of supply from Nashville and to protect his Atlanta base once he captured the city. Sherman would need that supply line because North Georgia was foraged out. He could lose one-half of his army group to this dull work. That and the requirements of force protection on the march could so deplete Sherman's striking power that he might never splash into salt water. Confederate forces in Georgia might just beat him.

Joe Johnston also was given three tasks by his national command authority. Resist Sherman's ambitions by helping Sherman run out of army before reaching Atlanta, keep Sherman away from Lee, and recover Tennessee for the Confederacy. In this way, Johnston along with Lee would "derange" Northern plans "and embarrass them the whole summer" leading to the fall elections.[48] Tennessee was the avenue down which Federal power could stab the Confederacy to the heart and up which Confederate power could threaten to cut in half the rump United States. Tennessee had been lost to the South after Grant expelled the Army of Tennessee under Braxton Bragg from the state in the battle of Chattanooga in late 1863. Davis wanted it back.

On March 5, 1864, Davis and his now military chief of staff Braxton Bragg called on Johnston and Longstreet, detached from Lee for service in East Tennessee, to drive north a Middle Tennessee campaign to recover the state. Johnston argued for delay to make the campaign's kick off coincide with the opening of the Northern electoral campaign in early summer. He proposed luring Sherman from his Nashville base to wreck him and liberate Tennessee. The glory won by Johnston's victorious soldiers would pull to the colors the fresh young manhood of Tennessee. Then Johnston's reinforced army would march north to throw the frighteners into Northern voters from Chicago to Boston and cast the South's decisive vote against Lincoln.

This plan, launched across sympathetic territory in Tennessee, had a greater chance of success than Sherman's lonely penetration through hostile Georgia. It was the Confederate plan the Federals expected and Grant feared.

The campaign began as Johnston had intended. Sherman came out of his base. Johnston fell back into the Confederate stronghold, making a long defense to Atlanta. Johnston gained strength with each backward mile as Sherman lost strength. The moment was sure to come, said Johnston, when "we could reasonably have expected to cope with the Federal army on equal ground."[49] At that moment, he said, he would attack, cut up, starve, annihilate Sherman's armies and push past their wreckage into Tennessee. Then

Johnston would be free to do whatever he pleased. Even cross the Ohio River, torch Chicago, and win the war.

Hungry to bring on this vast turning point, the Confederacy mustered all available troops to Johnston – more than 70,000 after the arrival of Leonidas Polk's forces from Mississippi. Richmond authorized Johnston to draw on over 91,000 effectives from all of the Western commands, South Carolina, and Georgia. But Johnston's capacity to call in so many troops was limited by their distance from the campaign scene and by the problem of prying them loose from jealous and parochial commanders.[50] Nevertheless, Johnston estimated his army and Sherman's at about the same size and that only a little time and attrition would bring on the turning point Johnston sought.

Johnston's army opened the fight like a vast guerilla force, fluid, fast, full of unhappy surprises, shadowing the Federal armies to strike at moments of weakness, then pulling away quickly to maneuver for another strike or a momentary holding action that would lead to a fresh attack in an unexpected place. In seventy-four days of non-stop combat – skirmishes with the occasional battle, each side raiding against, destroying, and rebuilding the Nashville-to-Atlanta rail line they both used for supply, both generals fighting with extreme care to conserve their regiments – Johnston slowed Sherman's advance to less than two miles a day when an infantry column could expect to march fifteen. Johnston was the only Confederate commander to slow a Sherman advance. "They don't drive worth a damn," Sherman's troops grumbled of the Army of Tennessee.[51] All this was a tremendous achievement in light of Johnston's grotesque underestimation of Federal numbers.

Johnston's "digging and retreating" campaign, as his soldiers called it, and the rugged terrain of north Georgia whittled down Federal strength. Sherman expended vast resources to maneuver against Johnston's lines only to find Confederate trenches empty and Johnston gone away "in one of his clean retreats."[52] When Johnston fought, he fought from heavy entrenchments built by contract slave labor and made Sherman pay the bill. At the Battle of Kennesaw Mountain, Johnston killed and wounded 3,000 blue for 600 gray. There, Hood counterattacked Joe Hooker's corps with such ferocity that Sherman had to rescue Fighting Joe from his own confusion and send him away, humiliated and angry, to resign. Kennesaw Mountain was the last frontal assault Sherman ever made against Johnston.

Johnston wrecked the country ahead of Sherman and scavenged it out, making Sherman doubly dependent on his fragile rail link to Nashville which Johnston was determined to break. As Sherman repeatedly failed to outflank Johnston, Johnston led him deeper into the South, making him more isolated and vulnerable each day, and bringing nearer the inevitable turning point of retribution. Johnston's strategy was working. He must have felt an anxious excitement for the approaching triumph that would crush Sherman as well as all those in Richmond who despised Johnston and whom he despised.

But there were potholes – no, craters – in Johnston's glory road. His plan was succeeding, but he was failing with his troops, his corps commanders, and his political masters. First, morale. Johnston was the Confederacy's "G.I. general," the man who had rescued this Army of Tennessee from the starvation, despair, and failure of its previous commander, Braxton Bragg. He was "Uncle Joe" whom his men knew never would risk their lives in pointless battle. But Johnston was no more willing to communicate the essence of his campaign plan to his soldiers than he was to describe it to his president. To the men in their defensive trenches and on their retreating marches, this fallback campaign began to look like failure. Johnston was losing the confidence of his army.

Second, the fights Johnston won over Sherman were too often scotched by Johnston's hesitant subordinates, their lack of senior command experience, and an inept Hood. These were men foisted on Johnston by Davis when the president refused all of Johnston's choices for corps commanders. Johnston knew their inadequacies. He also knew he had no leisure to train them up in the middle of this campaign. He had to use them to the full of their limited capacities and then himself fill in for their limitations. But he could not command the army and each of its corps, as well.

Third, although Johnston was running out the war to the North's Election Day, he could not find that promised moment of numerical superiority allowing him to launch his crushing counterattack on Sherman. He could whip Sherman at Kennesaw Mountain but he could not throw him out of Georgia. He could find no turning point because Sherman fought so carefully. And because Sherman – powered by his fierce and itchy temper and the dread burden knowing Grant's war plan now depended on him – drove forward against Johnston with a relentlessness new to the Confederate experience of Federal commanders.

The moment finally came at the outskirts of Atlanta when Johnston realized there would be no turning point for him. He had underestimated by half the size of Sherman's forces and he could not beat them. In the shimmering heat and dust of August, less than three months after opening his campaign to recover Tennessee, Joe Johnston sent his troops scrambling into the slave-built trench line around Atlanta. The war of 1864's second great siege, and even more politically important stalemate, began.

The Confederate government had squandered the seventy-four days Johnston had bought for it in his fallback campaign. Richmond failed to use that time to plot a fresh road to victory. Richmond had devised no new war plan to confront the North's new strategy, built no wonder of trans-Atlantic political negotiation, made no alliance with French

Mexico to allow a pouring across the Texas border of Imperial regiments. There was to be no conjuring new armies out of the 100,000 men who had deserted the Stars and Bars or recruited out of the mixed-bloods of the Southwest and southern California, places inclined toward the Confederacy but so far away they thought this civil war a foreign affair. Richmond was empty, exhausted, intellectually beaten before the ground war was over. The men who had begun the war in 1861 still ran the war. No new blood, no new thinking.

The full burden of winning the Confederate war now fell on Johnston. He never expected to be driven back on Atlanta, duplicating the mess Lee had made in Virginia. He had no plan to fight out of a besieged Atlanta. His army was depleted in *materiél* and morale. Richmond had no more men and supplies to give him. But if Johnston could stall Sherman as Lee was stalling Grant, then stalemate east and west could shift Northern frustration toward votes for a peace candidate to end the war.

Grant agreed: "For my own part, I think that Johnston's tactics were right," he wrote in his *Memoirs*. "Anything that could have prolonged the war a year beyond the time that it did finally close, would probably have exhausted the North to such an extent that they might then have abandoned the contest and agreed to a separation."[53] Johnston's campaign and the developing siege at Atlanta kept alive the chance for Confederate victory. But the Confederate government was about to throw it away.

* * *

DECISION FOR A NEW HORSE IN MID-STREAM

In the West, two conservative generals had fought a low-risk, low-casualty campaign so not to lose the war while in the East two radical generals fought a fast, bludgeoning campaign for victory in which lives seemed to count for nothing at all. The results East and West were the same. Stalemate. But, because the calendar now ran faster toward Northern Election Day, the siege of Atlanta gave advantage to the Confederacy. That is not how the government and people of the South saw it.

Terrified and despairing Southerners called Johnston "The Great Retreater" and saw his failure to destroy Sherman as pushing the Confederacy toward disaster. Could this man be a closet Lincolnite or insufficiently Southern or, as the newspapers had begun to rage, unmanly and a coward? Governor Joe Brown, ever ready to secede from secession into his own "Republic of Georgia," raved against a Southern confederacy that could not spare Georgia from Sherman.[54] The hard-bitten rebels in the national leadership who expected to hang on Yankee gallows if Johnston lost the war blamed him for "a disastrous loss of territory" that drove down Southern morale.

Richmond expected Johnston to send the massed cavalry it would not provide him to sweep behind Federal lines to cut the railroad and maroon Sherman to starve in Georgia while the massed infantry no adjacent commanders would send him bashed through Sherman's front. If not that, then Richmond expected Johnston to withdraw west, luring Sherman away from Georgia's farms and arsenals and into the less vital territory of Alabama, and join with Lieutenant General Richard Taylor's troops in Mobile to annihilate Sherman. Richmond expected Johnston to do all his with a rough-riding Southern boldness instead of his usual cold calculation.

When Johnston undertook neither of these options, Richmond was appalled. His government should have been more dismayed that Johnston had no plan prepared for what he would do after he had been thrown back on Atlanta. He appeared to Richmond ready to abandon the city, believing the Confederacy needed his living army more than it needed any living city, regardless of the city's political and economic value. Davis, desperate and once again ill – his was a double war against the North and against his own wretched health – and in a high frenzy, called Johnston a traitor and that closed the case against the general. The president's cabinet unanimously called for Johnston's removal.

Jefferson Davis was pleased to oblige but, as a good democrat in a highly factionalized political system and with a politician's worry for his popularity, Davis had to perform a soft shoe of seeming deliberation and fairness before cashiering Johnston and reaching down the seniority ladder to raise up John Bell Hood as the Confederacy's youngest and least experienced army commander.

While Davis and his faction fought off the political support rallying to Johnston's defense, Davis packed off to Atlanta his military chief of staff, Braxton Bragg, to report the situation on the ground and consulted Lee for the military's opinion on what was to be done.[55] On July 12, Davis wrote Lee that "General Johnston has failed, and there are strong indications that he will abandon Atlanta....It seems necessary to me to relieve him at once. Who should succeed him? What think you of Hood for the position?"[56]

Lee's two reserved replies were politically aware, self-protective, and resigned to what Lee knew Davis intended to do. At 8:45 P.M. on July 12 Lee telegraphed Davis, saying, "It is a bad time to release [relieve] the commander of an army situated as that of Tenne. We may lose Atlanta and the army too. Hood is a bold fighter. I am doubtful as to other qualities necessary." Lee followed this with a letter to Davis written at 9:30 P.M., saying, "I am distressed at the intelligence conveyed in your telegram of today. It is a grievous thing to change commander of an army situated as that of the Tennessee. Still if necessary it ought to be done. I know nothing of the necessity. I had hoped that Johnston was strong enough to deliver battle....Hood is a good fighter very industrious on the battle field, careless off & I have had no opportunity of judging his action, when the whole responsibility rested upon him. I have a high opinion of his gallantry, earnestness & zeal. Genl Hardee has more experience managing an army."[57]

Next day, Braxton Bragg arrived in besieged Atlanta after a high profile meander through the war-torn Confederacy consulting with politicians and commanders along his route to prepare the political ground for Johnston's removal. On July 14, Bragg held two meetings with Johnston that can only be described as fantastic. Standing there at ground zero of a developing military disaster, the two generals discussed the military situation but refused to sweat out what was to be done to save Atlanta. That is confirmed by contemporary witnesses and post-war testimony from each of them. Johnston was suspicious of Bragg. Bragg acted like a man ticket-punching for a decision already made. Now, as part of the visit's orchestration, Bragg received a letter from Hood, saying, "I have, general, so often urged that we should force the enemy to give us battle as to almost be regarded reckless by the officers high in rank in this army, since their views have been so directly opposite."[58]

Bragg had found at Atlanta what he had been sent to find – an army commander so focused on the military picture he was unwilling to preserve Atlanta with all its political and economic value because he wanted his army free to attack the enemy army from all points. But how could Johnston's army of merry free-rangers survive if he gave up the Atlanta Arsenal, its principal weapons supplier? How could the Confederacy fight on without Atlanta's transportation nexus to the Georgia-Alabama mining, industrial, and agricultural heartland? How could Georgia continue to arm and feed Lee's army facing Grant? To hold Atlanta, to stymie Sherman and Grant across the summer, meant the South could win the Northern election in November. To abandon Atlanta was to give up the war.

Bragg cabled Davis on July 15, "I cannot learn that he [Johnston] has any more plan for the future than he has had in the past,"[59] but happily I have found a suitable replacement anxious to fight for the city: "Hood," Bragg wrote in another message on July 15, "would give unlimited satisfaction." *Unlimited satisfaction.* What an absurd thing to say in a military message to a president. Here the message shifts from comic to grim as Bragg adds, "Do not understand me as proposing him as a man of genius, or a great general but as far better in the present emergency than any one we have *available.*"[60]

There is that word again – *available.* The key word in Bragg's message. Hood, dynamic but untested in army command, his battlefield mobility crippled by his wounds, mooning over a girl back home, was all the hot-blooded, organization-scorning South and its feuding president had made available to themselves.

Yet Bragg, still smarting from his loss of the Army of Tennessee to Johnston, likely saw Hood as a marginal candidate whose hotly aggressive combat style could push the Confederacy past the immediate crisis but whose accumulation of error from his overall inadequacy soon enough would require his being superseded by a more solid man. By Braxton Bragg.

* * *

In that dank hour before midnight, Johnston read the order relieving him of command, promoting John Bell Hood to full general, and giving the Army of Tennessee to Hood. Johnston immediately published the order to the army, packed his kit, loaded his wagons, and, within twenty-four hours and without a farewell briefing to his successor, rode away to home and wife in Macon, Georgia, his military and political ambitions wrecked.[61]

The Richmond *Whig* cheered, saying, "Hood is young, dashing and lucky...[he will] drive back Sherman and save Atlanta."[62] But Hood was stunned by the enormity of the task he had grabbed. While Johnston packed his wagons, Hood, sounding very much like Lee, cabled Davis to say, "I deem it dangerous to change the commanders of this army at this particular time, and to be to the interest of the service that no change should be made until the fate of Atlanta is decided." *Assuming army command would be so much sweeter, he* seemed to say, *if Johnston would take the blame for losing Atlanta.* Davis irritably and curtly refused Hood's request to delay the order.[63]

But rabid secessionists, horrified at the rapidly shortening Northern election calendar, turned on Davis: *Why did the one-eyed old fool give our last army to this rash young man who never commanded a battle? This is madness! Madness loses the war and gets us all hanged. Rescind the appointment!* But Davis would not change his mind. He was too proud and obstinate ever to yield to any opposition, his wife Varina testified. He stuck to friends even when proved wrong. He refused to be contradicted in his opinions.[64] He remained an unrepentant Confederate until he died in 1889, the last twenty-four years of national peace for him merely a pause while the South searched for a new hero to rally fresh armies to renew the Civil War. Davis would stick with Hood down the road to Hell to scorn all their enemies.

This rigid man and truest of friends also would make Hood stick to the bargain that had given him army command. Because to survive as president and survive the war, Davis needed Hood to save the Confederacy.

* * *

Sherman crowed that Hood in command at Atlanta "was just what we wanted." But Major General John A. Schofield, Hood's West Point roommate, warned Sherman, "He'll hit you like h--l, now, before you know it."[65] Sherman was never happy doing what he was doing today, always hungry to move on to the next thing and then hurry on to the thing after that. He had not yet won Atlanta but already he was surveying a march route to the sea. He recognized Hood as a risk to that plan because whatever Hood might choose to do next was unpredictable and Sherman did not like the unpredictable.

If Sherman was amused to face Hood as his competitor for Atlanta, Sherman knew he faced hard fighting and the unhappy unexpected. Hood was too much an opportunist and too little a method fighter to think to force Sherman "to run up against prepared intrenchments" as had Johnston.[66] There would be no more Kennesaw Mountains, no stand-up fighting across a trench line. Instead, there would be army-size Indian warfare all across Georgia and the dread unpredictable. Hood would strike from here and there, all swirling feathers and zipping lead, and he would hit hard because he feared nothing for himself or his army. That had to worry Sherman because it worried the stone-cut man Grant who stood behind him. *Now*, Sherman wrote his wife, *the war begins*.

Hood prowled around Atlanta watching for a Sherman misstep. The huge Federal army group was slow to maneuver, moving in multiple columns so tempting for attack in detail. The Army of Tennessee was compact, agile, and quick. Tiger against elephant. Hood was a natural at getting inside what the conceptual father of Operation Desert Storm in Iraq, John Boyd, called his enemy's "OODA Loop" – Observation, Orientation, Decision, Action – to recognize opportunity first and act faster with greater unpredictability than the enemy and to keep doing it until the enemy was shattered. But the size of Sherman's total force was a protection in itself and Sherman was a weird new factor. He was wild with energy and fiercely determined, so unlike Union generals before 1864. Sherman absorbed each of Hood's surprise assaults and, by skill, luck, and because he had better, more experienced subordinate generals, threw back and counterattacked Hood. The elephant shook off the tiger and stomped him.

Hood lost each of the battles he made around Atlanta, costing him forty percent of his troops – more per campaign day than Johnston had lost and more in total than Lee had sacrificed at Gettysburg. Hood cost Sherman's 85,000 blue soldiers engaged a casualty list of 32,000 killed, wounded or missing. But he cost his own army more. Of Hood's 65,000 engaged, 35,000 were shot out of the war or captured and imprisoned.[67] Yet Hood was making the rabidly aggressive fight for which his president chose him. The newspapers loved it. War-weary Southern people cheered.

But their president began to weigh Hood's startling losses – the growing lists of dead and wounded, of supplies torched, of farms trampled, of slaves run off, of Atlanta buildings blown to bits by Sherman's artillery, of women and children flung adrift and starving in a withering city and along country roads – against the limited impact Hood had on Sherman and his plans. It was too late in the war for all this waste without a better return. The national wealth to be spent for independence was running out. Jefferson Davis began to doubt his champion. He never doubted his decision to create that champion or to order him to do that which Davis had ordered. But he began to doubt Hood as he had come to doubt every other general he had sent to command the Army of Tennessee.

Yet Hood as commander performed well at Atlanta. He was an opportunistic tactician in the Lee mold. He showed himself better in independent command than Lee's great lieutenant, Longstreet. Winning battles is about achieving unfair advantage. Hood watched for opportunity to concentrate against a weaker target force. He struck fast, hit hard, crashing into blue elements in flank or in motion or unentrenched. He caught Sherman's forces in the open, overconfident, poorly organized, badly distributed through field and forest. He intended to break up each of the separate components of Sherman's army group in order to drive the whole into demoralized ruin, reeling and weeping up the rail line to Nashville. That was a reasonable plan.

Looking at the intelligence Hood had available to him and at the too many opportunities Sherman gave him as he maneuvered his large and complex army to strangle the city, it is evident Hood analyzed well the combat problems he faced, devised sound plans to convert those problems into victories, and sent his forces down the right roads into fights they could win. But Hood's combat luck had run out. There was to be no repeat of Chickamauga, no happy accident of bungled Union maneuvers allowing Hood to spur his hellions in a battle-winning wedge through the center of this blue army. There was to be no such thing because Johnston's long fallback had convinced Sherman's troops, down to the weakest-kneed private and weediest drummer boy, that they were war-winners. Here, in this fighting in Georgia against this madman Hood, they would win the war, open the slave-free future, put the nation right with God, and restore the Union. They believed themselves the great blue tide that would not recede until it had drowned every gray thing in its way.

Their generals, lashed forward by that furious redhead, used these willing men to make quick and agile support of one another, to plug their commander's mistakes in maneuver and planning. There were breaks in Sherman's army, glaring errors of march and maneuver, and Hood happily invaded to exploit them. But Sherman had good men for lieutenants, as good and brave as the good, brave men they commanded. These lieutenants closed the gaps Sherman made. The soldiers fought away their commander's errors. And no one in blue would yield to Hood. That is why Hood's luck had run out.

Hood continued to make heroic war. His battles around Atlanta raised hopes in Richmond and cheers from the newspapers. But the president who had hired him for attack became so dismayed at the disproportionate and unrecoverable losses in troops that he ordered Hood to cease and desist and fall back on the city.

* * *

The End at Atlanta

Hood withdrew into Atlanta's fortifications and Sherman promptly came up and bombarded the city. This was not the London blitz but awful just the same. Shockingly so for people unprepared for anything so terrible as endless numbers of enemy bombs whistling down day and night to fire houses and throw their walls into roadways, gouge shell craters, crush vehicles and gut horses, slaughter screaming women and children and strew their corpses in plain sight, and invite into the death-stinking city flies big as thumbs to gorge on pooled blood. It was "painful, yet strange, to mark how expert grew the old men, women and children, in building their little underground forts, in which to fly for safety during the storm of shell and shot," said Hood.[68] Behind this artillery barrage, and fending off each of Hood's infantry assaults, Sherman surrounded the city and cut its rail lifelines.

At 5:00 P.M. on September 1, Hood began evacuating Atlanta to save his army. Around midnight, his rearguard torched his trainload of powder, shot, shell, and other supplies because he could not get the train out of the city past Sherman's pincers. This was an act of astonishing miscalculation. The rail yard shot up a gout of orange and red and the shattering roar of the first explosion must have seemed to the last denizens of the city, cowering in their "dungeons beneath the earth," like the herald of the world's utter destruction. The blasts throbbed through the night air and shook the earth far beyond Atlanta so that Federal soldiers closing in on the city cheered, thinking, *My God, have we just won the war and I'm still alive?*

Next morning, when the last round had cooked off in the ruins of the train yard but with buildings still burning and not enough strong men to shovel dirt over the flames, Mayor James M. Calhoun surrendered the city to Major General Henry W. Slocum, United States Army. "The enemy entered Atlanta at 11 a.m. yesterday with colors flying and bands playing."[69] The North's most critical military achievement of 1864 had been accomplished.

Hood left Atlanta with 40,403 weary troops while across the combat line Sherman subdivided Grant's "spare army" to take his best 62,000 men on a picnic across Georgia. Sherman sent the leftovers – his second best soldiers with the sick and walking wounded – up the rail line toward Nashville and Union Major General George H. Thomas.

Three days after Atlanta's fall, Hood wrote Bragg, "I think the officers and men of this army feel that every effort was made to hold Atlanta to the last. I do not think the army is discouraged."[70] But the casualty toll in Georgia was disproportionately against the South. Sixty percent of all casualties in the Johnston fallback/Hood Atlanta campaigns were lost under Hood's command.[71]

Now it was Hood's turn to take the scorn of press and public. One more glittering knight unmasked as a stumblebum. As bad – no, worse! – than the old fogies of Johnston, Lee, and Beauregard whom his new young breed was meant to displace and outpace.

With Richmond in bickering confusion, the press rabid, and the population confounded, Hood suddenly found himself freed of unrealistic expectation. Free to move and fight his army as military commanders usually are most pleased to do – without the responsibility of doing anything but fighting. Hood could prosecute the Western war pretty much as he liked. He was free to be Hood and free to take the tough and powerful Army of Tennessee with him. Hood set out once again to win the war. But had to win back his army first.

* * *

The Army of Tennessee mutinied against Hood. Not in total but in significant parts. This was an army that had refused or thrown off previous commanders. After the Atlanta debacle, the army wanted rid of Hood. A good general does not waste his soldiers' lives but finds them victories worthy of sacrifice. Hood spent soldier lives at Atlanta for no victory. His soldiers wanted better. Mutiny demanded the curative power of the Confederate president to restore the army to its commander.

Hood's corps commanders appealed to Davis to return Johnston to command. They seemed to forget their harsh complaints that Johnston's fallback campaign had broken army morale. Or perhaps, after their experience of the wild man Hood, a Joe Johnston war of balance and maneuver with limited dying looked just about right to them. On his fallback campaign, Johnston inflicted sixty percent more losses on Sherman for half the casualty rate of Hood's Atlanta fiasco.[72] Still, it is incredible to think these generals had no idea how absurd Davis must have regarded their petition.

His travel to the army must have been an infuriating chore for Davis. Once more he had to sort out Tennessee when Northern Virginia just kept banging along. Travel was complicated by risk of capture by Federal raiders. By tiresome and repeated delays on the war-battered rail lines. By the outrage he felt in reading newspapers collected along the way in which Davis and Hood were violently "denounced throughout the South" for losing Atlanta.[73] When he reached the army, soldiers interrupted his September 25 speech to them shouting, "Johnston! Give us Johnston!"[74]

But the president showed himself as stoutly loyal to Hood as he always was to his friends or to any decision he made. He counterattacked his political enemies and the newspapers by denouncing both Joe Johnston and Georgia Governor Brown in terms so bitter and "unmeasured" that hearers thought he all but called them traitors to the Confederacy.[75] Then he appealed to the corps commanders and to the army to stand by Hood.

Hood offered to resign the command not because of the disapproval of his corps commanders and soldiers but because he seems to have been rattled by a bad press. That was a new experience for Hood. He was shocked to be the target of so much public outrage. He also knew Lee had submitted his resignation after Gettysburg and had seen that a commander's offer of resignation could be an effective public relations ploy. It would begin to redeem Hood among his and Davis's political supporters. Its nobility would restore him in the eyes of the girl he had left back home. A resignation refused would share out the blame for Atlanta and for any errors that might come next. Hood also knew he had Davis in a vise grip of the old man's unyielding loyalty and refusal to admit error. A resignation offer was low risk, high gain for Hood.

There, beside his resignation offer on the table, Hood spread out a map to present his president a bold new plan of action. He would, he said, lure the vile Sherman out of Georgia. Reconquer Tennessee. Take Kentucky. Drive 40,000 rifles burning across the peaceful farms and villages of the Ohio Valley. Even threaten to raise red battle flags on Chicago skyscrapers. Break up Grant's squeeze-'em-'til-they-burst strategy by luring him away from Richmond and free Lee to be as wild in the East as Hood would be in the West. The war would be renewed! For a Southern leadership made desperate by Grant's new style of war-making, this "was truly a cheerful & refreshing scheme to contemplate at the present stage of our affairs!!"[76] Besides, the operational plan was Davis's own idea, one he had long pushed but which no other Western general had thought worth taking up.

Here was dual opportunity for Davis. Take up the resignation letter and he would rid himself of a general who had wasted thousands of soldier lives and channel onto Hood the blast of public anger for the loss of Atlanta. A swift and confident dismissal would add to the president's prestige and political power, commodities in sharp decline after Atlanta. Ah, what a happy turnabout that would make! Yet this plan of Hood's promised once again all those things that a Hood in command of a great army could offer – startling hot action to please the newspapers, swift retribution to confound the president's political enemies, and a making of battles so wild that Sherman and all his horde could not contain them. For all the reasons Davis had appointed Hood in July, he kept Hood in command in September.

Davis overestimated the offensive capacity remaining in the Army of Tennessee. He underestimated the capacity of Sherman's army group. He underestimated Grant's new style of war-making. He refused to accept that sometimes one Southern boy cannot whip twice his weight in blue wildcats. He expected Hood's depleted army to recover Atlanta promptly, wreck Sherman while he was isolated in the Deep South – as the Russians had isolated and wrecked Napoleon, he said – and strike into the Ohio Valley to disrupt Grant's continental master plan. He expected Hood to set up the circumstances allowing Davis to find some new way to win the war.

In a cooler moment, Davis rethought his Hood problem and, on October 2, raised P. G. T. Beauregard out of his exile to uselessness to make him coordinator of the Military Division of the West. Beauregard could initiate no combat action but he would coordinate Hood's operations with those of Richard Taylor's 32,600 troops scattered across Alabama, Mississippi, and East Louisiana. Beauregard would provide Hood the experienced command advice and quality administrative support that Hood so evidently needed. Should Hood fail again, then Beauregard, another of the too many popular and political threats to Davis, would take the first arrows of blame. But Davis was convinced Hood would not fail. He was Hood, after all, and he had at his command a great army.

Now the war of 1864 began to take on a very strange character. The Confederate president believed Hood had sworn to draw Sherman out of Atlanta to destroy him from a "strong position in the mountains between Atlanta and Chattanooga" and that is what Davis immediately told reporters.[77] It was a good plan and Sherman said so, right after he read all about it in the Georgia newspapers. A day or so later, Lincoln caught up with the story in *The New York Times*.

Hood began to do as he had promised. Sherman began to respond as expected. Then Sherman stopped doing the expected and simply went away. Sherman made his great March to the Sea leaving Hood to withdraw into the forests of Alabama to prepare his Middle Tennessee campaign. Onlookers North and South were astonished to see these two great armies march away from each other, their generals racing after their separate ambitions.

The calendar finally ran out and the tectonic plates of the war shifted on Northern Election Day. After the Union armies and navy had delivered three great successes – Rear Admiral David Farragut captured Mobile Bay closing the South's last great port accessing the outside world, Major General Philip Sheridan cleared the Confederacy from the Shenandoah Valley and its repeated threats to Washington

City, and Sherman captured Atlanta – Lincoln was re-elected President. The Northern people had voted to fight on.

[Part III]

Hood's Odyssey of Battles

The truth so patent to us must ere long be forced upon the reluctant Northern mind. There are no vital points on the preservation of which the continued existence of the Confederacy depends. There is no military success of the enemy which can accomplish its destruction. Not the fall of Richmond, nor Wilmington, nor Mobile, nor Savannah, nor of all combined, can save the enemy from the constant and exhaustive drain of blood and treasure which must continue until he shall discover that no peace is attainable unless based on the recognition of our indefeasible rights.

– Jefferson Davis to the Confederate Congress,
November 7, 1864[78]

ON NOVEMBER 17, 1864, EARLY IN THE MORNING, Sherman and 62,000 of his toughest soldiers disappeared over the eastern horizon, gone from the view of Atlanta and

Confederate calculations, loose in the South's soft under-belly. The great March to the Sea had begun. *I trust,* Sherman wrote Grant, filled with a happy fury for revenge against Confederate disturbers of good order, *that the Richmond papers will keep you well-advised of my whereabouts.* Then Sherman began a colossal burning and smashing of Georgia to put himself on page one.

Hood, his scheme to neutralize Sherman in the West a failure, curled up to brood in his Alabama camps, waiting for shoes, gunpowder, more cavalry, and all the other things he needed to campaign through Tennessee.

Sherman sent Major General George H. Thomas to Nash-ville to block Hood's northern drive and to tease the Army of Tennessee away from Sherman's line of march so as not to spoil the riotous good fun for Uncle Billy's chosen boys. Oh, and Thomas also must keep Hood from linking up with Lee to whip Grant. As armament against Hood's army, now grown to 50,000 men, Sherman gave Thomas his second-best veterans – those not sound enough for the great march to saltwater – and John Schofield with two of the three corps of his Army of the Ohio, 22,000 men. This was disrespecting Hood's wild card power. Grant was startled and unhappy with Sherman's arrangements but let Sherman career off on his wild march for its paramount importance in burning out the South's capacity to continue the war.

Hood never before had organized a campaign. He had no plan for Tennessee. So far as can be determined, he had no detailed understanding of how to get 50,000 men and all their animals, supplies, and equipment from Alabama to

Nashville and beyond except to march them there, shoving the cavalry up front and dragging guns and wagons behind. He gave no written plan to his lieutenants. He expected them to know what to do or to improvise. After three years in command of combat units, Hood had not learned the clerical task of finding 50,000 pairs of shoes to put on 50,000 pairs of feet, finding forty rounds for each soldier's pocket, barrels of grease for the wagon wheels that haul the artillery, canvas tents against winter's rain and ice, cooking lard, rules for scavenging friendly country, courts-martial to shoot rapists and deserters, and a combat-loss excess of battle flags, signal mirrors, frying pans, horseshoes, all of it.

While the Confederate Ordnance Department and Hood's quartermasters hastily piled up the army's supplies, Jefferson Davis brooded on a Middle Tennessee campaign that could not be allowed to become just one more Pennsylvania-style raid. No half-success this time. Hood on this raid into the North had to out-do Lee. He had to break open the war. Retaking Tennessee meant nothing in deflecting Grant's continental strategy. Hood had to plant his battle flags on free soil, splitting – or threatening to split – the West from the North to terrify the Northern public, if he was to accomplish anything at all. Divide the union of North and West and the war could be won despite a re-elected Lincoln and the newly professed hard-war and abolitionist will of the Northern people.

Beauregard, the godfather of the Western theater whom war's disappointments had made a realist, had no faith in the Middle Tennessee campaign. He believed Hood's army should have stuck to Sherman. Followed Sherman across Georgia, tearing away at Uncle Billy's bummers to deny the wild redhead his chance to bring his wreckers and looters under the protective rifles of the U.S. Colored Troops waiting to receive him on the coast beyond Savannah. Followed and depleted and slaughtered the bummers and left any survivors to the mercy of Georgia guerillas. Then Hood could turn his victorious army toward Richmond and Lee to combine the Western and Eastern armies for decisive battle against Grant. That was the main chance.

But Beauregard counted the 275 miles of devastated country now separating Hood and Sherman. A country of broken rail lines – broken by both armies – and burnt bridges, trampled fields, granaries emptied, no scavenge, no fodder, little support from a battered, sullen, and accusing Georgia population. No, Hood could not catch up to Sherman across all that, not before Sherman reached the sea and the protection of those black riflemen with the guns of the Federal navy behind them. Hood had let Sherman escape. Georgia was to be burnt out, the salt of failure plowed into its soil, and Beauregard had no means to stop it.

As bad, Sherman's march to the sea had nailed Hood and the Army of Tennessee to the Federal bullseye. Even if Beauregard could pull Hood back into Georgia, what would that do but open Alabama to invasion by George Thomas? Worse, Confederate desertions reached fifty-three percent in 1864 with over 120,000 men absent without leave from all Confederate armies.[79] Order this Tennessee army once more to march away from its home state for the sake of the half-loyal Confederates of Georgia and the army could dissolve.

Beauregard decided that pushing forward Hood's campaign was a better use of the Confederacy's dwindling resources until someone somewhere came up with a plan to win the war. Key to Beauregard's decision, however, was more failure of Confederate intelligence. Beauregard thought Sherman's army of bummers half as big as it was. He believed the 29,000 Confederate troops and Georgia militia available in the state – though many of the militia were old men, young boys, and derelicts – sufficient to "insure the destruction of Sherman's army, estimated by me at about 36,000..." But Georgians were war-weary and fewer than half the men Beauregard expected rallied to the flag. He had overestimated Georgia as he had underestimated Sherman. "The fate of the country," he now said, despondent, "may depend upon the results of Hood's campaign..."[80]

* * *

When Hood finally showed his Middle Tennessee campaign plan to Beauregard on October 20, a month before Sherman began his March to the Sea, Beauregard was appalled. Yes, Hood proposed to reconquer Tennessee to position his army to break out in any direction to do whatever was needed to reshape the war for the South and that was good. But he made no provision for logistical support, performed no intelligence surveys, had no clear understanding of his route of march. He had not even found for himself a good map of the country. Hood was preparing to march blind into Tennessee. Fixing all those problems for Hood was why Beauregard was made coordinator in the West and he would have to do all those things for Hood. But what had Hood learned about his enemy? What strength had George Thomas in Nashville, straddling Hood's route into the Ohio Valley? What could Thomas do with those forces? What additional power had Sherman sent Thomas before leaving on his march? Hood had no answers. But he was confident he knew enough to open his campaign.

In the struggle around Atlanta, Hood thought he knew "nigh every important movement of the enemy – through the vigilance of our cavalry, spies, and scouts, and from the information received through Federal prisoners."[81] But the facts are different. Hood's intelligence service repeatedly reported Sherman in retreat when Sherman was preparing to strike. Hood ignored this history of failure. Had Hood's scouts, spies, and cavalry merely harvested the vast amount of intelligence available to them from the pro-Confederate population of Nashville, they would have told their general that Federal forces in the city were too few and too disorganized to make a good fight. That an immediate assault, even half-prepared, could capture Nashville's supply stores as the launching pad for Hood's next great push. But that is not what happened.

Instead came the great waiting. A month without action on a calendar that begged for speed to achieve a victory before winter froze all hopes. The story from the record is that Hood in Tuscumbia, Alabama, delayed his campaign kickoff for a month as he drifted through the irritating confusions of logistical planning and as he played hide-and-seek with Beauregard to avoid hearing the man's too many criticisms of Hood's campaign planning. True enough. But the truer story, in a few lines of his autobiography, offers something bizarre. Hood had contrived a grand fantasy of heroic self-redemption.

Some historians think Hood stepped across into Tennessee with no campaign plan whatsoever but he had two plans. First, the combat plan he had sold to Davis and shown to Beauregard. And, second, another plan he could reveal to no one, a plan out of Edgar Allan Poe's "haunted palace" where a man or woman can dream the fantastic to oppose a terrible reality. In this plan, Hood would march through Tennessee scattering and destroying isolated Federal units before George Thomas at Nashville could concentrate forces. He would capture Nashville. Then, feeding off Nashville's rich stores and all those delicious Spencer repeating rifles and carbines stocked there – weapons that could make one soldier the equal of seven on the firing line and Hood's army of 50,000 men equal to anything Grant could send against it – he would sweep not into the Ohio Valley but drive east through Richmond's back door to rescue Lee! Destroy Grant! And idol and acolyte would lead Tennessee and Northern Virginia as one grand army of the Confederate republic into Washington City to win the war.[82]

A bizarre dream, yes, but the kind of dream a berserker general like Hood leading the tough Army of Tennessee could make real.

* * *

THE HARROWING OF THE GENERAL COMMANDING

Hood's campaign needed quick action and sharp maneuver to compensate for his lack of resources and to conquer Nashville before the whirling in of winter's sleet and ice. But Grant's logistical war and Sherman's capture of the Atlanta Arsenal had crippled the Confederate capacity to prepare Hood's army.

Some of Hood's supplies came from the hard-pressed Lee, a man notorious for not giving up a single bullet or soldier he believed better spent by himself. Hood waited for Lee to relent. Hood made poor choice of his successive bases. That complicated getting supplies to him. He waited while the Ordnance Department caught up. He called for cavalry and was promised it first from one source and then another. He waited some more. He needed the reopening of the Memphis and Charleston railroad to supply his troops on the march, a line he had wrecked in his "scorched iron" policy to deny the rails to a pursuing Sherman. He waited for repairs. He watched and worried about Sherman's capacity to return and interdict his campaign plan. His army, bored and sullen in camp, consumed the provisions Beauregard had sent for its march north. Hood had to wait for replacement supplies. He waited out one delay and that led to a new problem and another delay and on and on until this man of action and dream was so stricken with logistical problems, so driven to frustration, a Gulliver staked down by tiresome details, that he was nearly paralyzed.

George Thomas, a hundred miles north, faced a similar set of problems and threats of delay. But he took an adjutant's joy in them, a pleasure in the laborious solving of many little problems to produce one grand result. He was a man who liked to be well-prepared. To count all his men on the firing line before he would let them shoot and to dress his reserves in good new uniforms with plenty of brass buttons. To find horses for every one of his cavalrymen mooning about because they had none and train those horses and find saddles and bridles for them. And to issue out his Spencer repeaters and combat rations and build stouter his defensive walls.

Thomas did all of that in a kind of command frenzy because he knew he did not have fighting men the equal of those in the Army of Tennessee. He had a base full of cooks, clerks, green recruits, and bounty-jumpers dragged back to the army. Basecamp troopers who for months had done no more than march sentry duty around supply sheds or along rail lines. They were out of the habit of battle. He needed to fill the river behind the city with gunboats as his fallback line, but where were they? He had a city full of secessionists, spies, and saboteurs for Hood. He had been forgotten by Sherman, who had gone off on his wild picnic. The Army of Tennessee was somewhere over the horizon, time was running out and "Old Pap" Thomas and his armed rabble were all that stood against Confederate victory in the West. Oh, yes, there was John Schofield out there with his 22,000 men shadowing Hood but what could anyone reasonably expect so few to do against Hood and the Army of Tennessee? It is easy to imagine Thomas lying in his blankets each night staring into the gloom wondering if he had done enough that day to prepare for the frightfulness coming his way. Wondering if anything he could do with men like these could be enough.

* * *

The Memphis and Charleston railroad reopened to Hood's supply trains on November 21 and that day Hood launched 50,000 troops into Tennessee. Morale in the army rose as it marched into its home state. The weather became a wretched misery, shifting from Indian summer to sleety winter and back again in the space of a day. Then stinging-cold wind. Swollen rivers. Roads so thick with icy mud that wagons sank axle-deep. The countryside all around war-impoverished. Soldiers who had cheered to swing up the roads of their native state slogged weary marches through sucking mud and finished their days stupefied with exhaustion. Yet even before Hood could arrange any significant combat action his march toward the Ohio – at the moment the United States Congress reconvened after the November election and before Sherman had gotten anywhere near salt water – was a sharp embarrassment for the Lincoln administration.[83]

Hood is the wildest of Lee's wild men, the newspapers reminded their readers. If that confounded Lieutenant General Jubal Early just a few months past could drive a gray army into the outskirts of Washington City and take pot-shots at the President watching from a barricade, despite all the protective might of Federal power, what horror might Hood create on the Ohio with Sherman gone away Lord knows where? Grant's strategy had won Atlanta, yes, but what was that strategy winning now?

From 1862, when Grant took Nashville and raised over it sea Captain Stephen Driver's antique twenty-four-starred "Old Glory," the city had been under Federal power. Now Grant would have to recall Sherman from his March to the Sea or divert troops from the Richmond siege to save Chicago's 60,000 terrified citizens and the West beyond. *Lee would escape Grant's trap! The war would go on and on!* Here, to the Radicals controlling the Joint Congressional Committee on the Conduct of the War, was more proof that the Great Ape and his picked butcher-chieftain had no brains for this job. The Committee – which Lee saluted as worth two divisions to the South – wanted vengeance before the fact. Hood was late striking into Tennessee but any time he chose was a bad time for Lincoln and Grant.

While blue commanders and their President were thinking about Hood, there is scant evidence Hood thought much about the Federal generals he proposed to attack. Schofield, his old West Point roommate, had 22,000 men following Hood. George Thomas, the soldier so stubborn that, once settled into his defensive perimeter at the Battle of Chicka-mauga, he could not be moved any more than could an out-cropping of rock though the rest of the Federal army dissolved around him, held Nashville.

Hood may have considered that he knew Schofield too well – a man puffed up, greedy for fame and promotion, but a very ordinary combat leader, a plodder. If Hood had no good map of the road north, why, he could just follow Schofield fleeing from Hood to Nashville! As for Old Pap Thomas, Hood may have thought him a stubborn fool who lacked the energy to counter the free-for-all Hood would bring down upon him. Let Thomas pretend to be a rock and Hood would chip him away to nothing! Neither commander was in Hood's dynamic league. Both were his waiting victims.

Now Thomas sent a message to Schofield with his 22,000, saying, *Stop shadowing Hood. Intercept and delay his advance. Strike him. Hold him. Keep him away from me until I am ready to fight him.* Schofield must have expected the order. But it had to have come as a cold fright to have it in his hand. What could he do so heavily outnumbered against Hood? To "intercept and delay" Hood was to tease the tiger. No, it was to be the monkey biting the tiger's tail.

Schofield had a good force, a proud force filled with the high octane of the Atlanta victory. But it was crazy for Thomas to think these 22,000 could do more than slow the gray horde's march more than a few hours before Hood's 50,000 hellhounds shot them all to pieces. Yet Schofield had his orders and what he made of them for Hood was a sprawling, brawling, gun-fighting road race to Nashville. It was Johnston's fallback campaign in reverse with Confederates pushing Federals who fought and fell back in abrupt clear-outs only to shape new ground from which to shoot and fall back again.

It was a nightmare in which the Federals, unable to shake the dreamy horror of the gray enemy clutching at their coat-tails, scrambled for Nashville while the Confederates, caught in breathless, stumbling overreach, found the war-winning victory just beyond their outstretched fingers.

*   *   *

No Federal commander ever had been ready for the fireball power of a Hood attack but George Thomas had to make himself ready. Too many of Thomas's veteran soldiers had furloughed home to vote for Lincoln and had not yet returned to Nashville. So he dragged army cooks from their kitchens, clerks from their stools, and raw recruits just off the trains to stand trembling behind new-built barricades waiting for the terrible sound of the Rebel keen telling them Hood had come to slaughter them all. He put this motley force under the combat command of a quartermaster general and an engineer. He hauled in his outlying garrisons, risking charges by Hood's cavalry on the rail lines, warehouses, and loyal Tennessee villages that supported Federal power.

Because Thomas was a rock that would not be moved from the place it had come to rest, he prepared no line of retreat for himself and his garrison. Instead, he put gunboats and two ironclads on the Cumberland River behind the city. *You may smash me,* Thomas was saying to Hood, *but your great army will die in the water under the guns of this little navy I leave behind, and you will not march into the North.*

Until all of this could be patched together, Thomas needed Schofield as Nashville's mobile outer wall of defense. Schofield, unhappy, outmatched, and, to his mind, woefully supported by Thomas and thrown by Sherman into an impossible situation, pricked at and was chased by Hood for eight days until, on the night of November 29, Hood had Schofield trapped at Spring Hill, Tennessee. Hood was about to cripple Federal power in the state and make Nashville easy pickings. "[I]n the morning," Hood told his generals, "we will have a surrender without a fight. We can sleep quiet to night."[84] But the night of November 29 proved the most peculiar of this increasingly strange campaign.

Hood had been up since three that morning, riding strapped in his saddle, maneuvering his forces with skill and style, both driving and driven, his mind a constant calculator of opportunity against risk, and he was exhausted. He ate a big meal. Had something to drink. At 9:00 P.M., he put himself between clean sheets – heavenly for a combat soldier – in a bed beside a good fire in the guest room of a farmer's house. Well after Hood had drifted off to sleep and out there across the combat line, beyond forest and drifting campfire smoke, somewhere around 3:00 A.M., Schofield's blue soldiers were rousted from their exhausted and uneasy slumbers and told to march. *March? In the middle of the night? March! Keep silent! But march!*

Individual gray generals and private soldiers drifted into Hood's sleeping room, each waking his commander to report signs and rumors that Schofield was on the move to somewhere else. Noises had been heard on the road going away – rattle of harness, thump of wagon wheels, Yankee accents. Flashes of light from smoking pipes, gleams on brass fittings. Bluecoats had wandered by mistake to Confederate campfires for warmth and coffee, and then fled away.

Sometime in that night, the exhausted Hood – bleary with sleep or alcohol or a dose of laudanum to ease residual pain from his old wounds – gave or thought he gave orders to seal off Schofield's escape route. But he gave the order to generals who were themselves as exhausted as he after eight days' marching and fighting. More exhausted from trying to survive in a clumsy and awkward command environment under a commanding general with no experience managing an army. After the army's outbursts at Palmetto – "Give us Johnston!" – and Davis's embarrassing interviews with Hood's subordinates, these generals knew they lacked their commander's confidence. After the loss of Atlanta and the unnecessary delay in Alabama forced this campaign into winter's icy blast, they lacked confidence in Hood. These generals were tired men, inexperienced in high combat command, uncertain about too many things for which they needed to be certain. They were unready to risk making a mistake.

Hood's order was confusing – seal off what escape route? Hadn't the commanding general gone to bed telling them Schofield was trapped and must capitulate at first light or be crushed? What did this order mean? Better not try to interpret the commanding general's order. Better no action tonight than the wrong action and the commander's acid denunciation tomorrow. *Let the general wake when he will and give us his order clearly. Until then, do nothing.* That is what they did – nothing.

Hood made no effort to assure his order was carried out. He had no chief of staff to do that for him nor did he assign another officer to track the action. He seems to have been stupefied with exhaustion and the repeated interruptions of his sleep. Hood slept and Schofield's little army night-marched away, marching for its life.

"It was the most critical time I have ever seen," said a Federal brigade commander: "If only the enemy had shown his usual boldness, I think he would have beaten us disastrously."[85] Hood wrote in his memoirs: "The Federals, with immense wagon trains, were permitted to march by us the remainder of the night, within gunshot of our lines. I could not succeed in arousing the troops to action, when one good division...could have routed...the enemy...Had I dreamed one moment that [corps commander Benjamin F.] Cheatham would have failed to give battle," Hood said he would have risen from his sleep to lead the charge himself. Next morning, Hood in wild exasperation cried, "General, why in the name of God have you not attacked the enemy, and taken possession of the pike?"[86]

Hood, throughout his brief career as army commander, repeatedly failed to follow up on the execution of his orders. The battles of Peachtree Creek and East Atlanta and the night of Spring Hill are the grossest examples. He did not closely supervise his corps commanders to press them to win the objectives he set for them. He modeled his management style on Lee, who withdrew from close supervision of his subordinate commanders to allow them freedom to get on with the work he had set them, in some cases giving poor generals the freedom to flounder and fail. But Lee had established in his army an ensemble of leadership in which he could have confidence, something Hood never achieved in the Army of Tennessee.

Nor did Hood have sufficient time in high command or personal capacity to learn from his mistaken approach to leadership. Worse, he was too physically crippled to get himself to critical points in a battle to direct it to success over the weaknesses of his subordinates. Despite the hellhound of failure snapping at his heels to urge him on, eight days' nonstop combat and command appear to have exhausted Hood beyond his capacity to perform his duty at Spring Hill.

There are conflicting reports about what happened when Hood woke next morning, November 30. The reports are partisan and strange and eyewitness accounts few. They all say that morning's meeting of the army's senior officers was one of rage, fury, and finger-pointing accusation, with fighting words such as "incompetence," "cowardice," and "lack of spirit."[87]

Sounding as petulant as a Captain Queeg, Hood later wrote, "I had been harshly judged and feebly sustained by officers and men," and he was right. He blamed the debacle on Cheatham and division commanders John C. Brown and Patrick R. Cleburne.[88] In that he also was right. But Hood had forgotten Murphy's First Law of Combat: If a battle order can be misunderstood, it will be, and the Light Brigade will charge in the wrong direction. Hood had failed his commander's duty to issue clear orders and to follow up every detail. He had let things go wrong. Spring Hill was his failure.

Hood in his fury determined to smash his enemies, gray and blue, to redeem his army and his reputation, to keep the girl back home and his chance for a glorious ascent into the Southern aristocracy. Now, with his army again chasing its blue enemy, Hood in his memoirs reported that a "sudden change in sentiment" gripped officers and men. A "general feeling of mortification and disappointment" called up a terrific yearning for redemptive action.[89] No other eyewitness records this sensation.

* * *

THE HARROWING OF THE ARMY OF TENNESSEE

Hood sent Major General Nathan Bedford Forrest's cavalry pounding out of Spring Hill to shove Schofield's march-weary troops into the village of Franklin, Tennessee, just one day's march south of Nashville. Forrest corralled the Federals and pushed them into old earthworks which the blue soldiers very hastily rebuilt and on which they piled twenty-eight artillery pieces. But that cold recitation of facts does not tell the pounding heart of the moment.

The key to it all lies in the number of guns. Sometimes guns are just tools on the battlefield. Sometimes they are something more. This was the moment when they were more. Without yet firing a shot, these twenty-eight guns sitting silent and facing into the gray horde hounding down upon them with yips and Rebel yells and sprays of lead said, *These blue men will not be moved.*

The artillery spoke not simply for their commanding general who, despite his being about to prove himself a good battle manager this day, had to have been filled with the soldier's fright of ghastly failure, of his country wounded, his commander's scorn, his family shamed, himself dead or crippled or starving in a Rebel prison or, worse, shunted away out of the war into humiliation. They spoke not just for the blue men and officers hastily in earnest fear lifting fresh log barricades into place and piling up berms of earth and cutting fields of fire. They also spoke for Grant's continental battle plan, for five blue arrows on a map, of a supreme commander who had a superstitious dread of ever going back up a road he had come down. All that made them twenty-eight guns that never would be moved. They would kill or die but they would not be moved. Unstoppable gray men had come up against unmovable blue iron.

Hood tried another end-run around Schofield to sweep up his little army. Hood moved his troops well, driving them forward with speed and foresight through forest and up rutted roads. His vanguard ran pounding and sweating after the fleeing blue coats just a few hundred yards up the road. In easy sight, within rifle range if anyone in gray could take the time to stop and fire. The first gray troops stumbling and inter-tangling with the tail end of the blue wagon train. But here now ended the fighting road race and something new and terrible began.

With cleverness and skill, Schofield had taken advantage of Hood's errors and the Army of Tennessee's poor internal coordination that resulted from the corps commanders' inexperience. Schofield had made few errors himself. He had managed, just barely, to keep his half-size army out of Hood's grasping reach. But now he had run out of maneuver space. He had a river to cross if he was to reach Nashville and the tiger was coming on with ground-sweeping speed, eyes agleam, fangs dripping. The moment called for heroism or disaster. Which would Schofield have?

* * *

No army in any age moves with absolute cohesion and Schofield's was no different. An army's core force with its flags, leading generals, and sleek mounts may go forward according to plan but subordinates mistake roads, men drift away to loot and sleep, cowards and goldbricks seek hideaways, wagons break axles and block the route, cavalry gallops this way instead of that, conflicting intelligence reports frighten some to inaction and impel others to strike out independently. To observe an army on the march is not to see a single-minded creature but an anarchist's delight, a thing that seems to be everywhere at once and nowhere in particular. It is an immense task for a commander to move an army from point to point with most of its component parts arriving approximately where and when they should. Hood solved this problem for Schofield. He scooped up Schofield's troops, scattered in their desperate tramp north, and tumbled them into the broken-down rifle pits and trenches of Franklin, another of the ancient battlefields of much fought-over Tennessee. Hood put behind them the obstacles of the town of Franklin and a bridgeless, swollen river. He sent out gray cavalry to seal flank escape routes. Hood shaped the battle he wanted to make. He also shaped Schofield's little force into a compact fighting mass and made it fiercely determined by making it desperate. Yankee soldiers looking out of their earthworks at all this must have thought, *So near Hood and so far from hope! What's left but to fight like hell?*

Hood had the blue enemy in his grip once again and this time Hood himself was there, awake, alert, no longer dependent on his sluggard lieutenants. Hood had Schofield on his bullseye. Breaking Schofield, the movable outer wall of the Nashville defenses, was the key to prosecuting all the rest of Hood's campaign. Destroy him and Nashville was easy pickings. What supreme satisfaction this moment must have been for Hood after so much disappointment. But Schofield, sullen and slippery, already had begun his next fighting getaway. His teamsters whipped on their horses hauling army wagons north across planks flung down on a railroad bridge over the Harpeth River, making one last furious sprint to Nashville and safety.

Hood lashed his, as he claimed, newly invigorated army at double-quick time toward Franklin and arrived outside the town to find Forrest and his other generals unwilling to attack. With scarcely controlled rage, Hood stood on Winstead Hill, gazing across two miles of open fields cut by the Columbia Pike toward Franklin and the old defenses, and heard his generals' arguments. Out there, at the far end of the field and on a small rise of ground, he could spot a single outpost of Federal troops in as ill-conceived a forward position as the Peach Orchard at Gettysburg. Those blue people over there had learned nothing. Schofield was showing himself a tactical fool. Behind this outpost, whose only contribution to the coming battle could be to lie down and die, Hood through his binoculars could watch blue men frantically digging deeper into the old trench lines or shoving artillery into battery. Hood could see that Schofield was outnumbered, flanked, driven in on himself, concentrated in those ruined works, well and truly caught and forced at last to make a stand up fight instead of one of his patented getaways. Hood would crush Schofield in this grave he was digging for himself. Here was the terrific moment!

Around Hood flowed the grand sight of the gray army taking position. Rifles gleaming, bands playing, Southern Cross battle flags uncased and rising up in the fields and among the trees, these the new battle flags issued to Joe Johnston on the eternal fallback to Atlanta. The original Southern Cross design had a field of pink silk because only whores wore red silk but war's lacks forced the flags Hood carried to be cotton and red. Now Hood's 50,000 American killers would march under an unchaste banner with intent to murder 22,000 of their American brothers.

Looking across these open fields toward the blue earthworks was not looking across the valley toward stout Union defenses on Cemetery Ridge at Gettysburg. But it was too nearly like it for Hood's generals. They were no more willing to step off Pickett-like against this position than Longstreet had been to send Pickett up Cemetery Ridge. The Franklin position, corps commander Stephen D. Lee wrote in his after-action report, "was, for infantry defense, one of the best I have ever seen."[90]

And then there were those twenty-eight guns. Federal artillery at Gettysburg had torn up Pickett's great charge on July 3, ripping apart the divisions of George Pickett, J. Johnston Pettigrew, and Isaac R. Trimble before their brave regiments could reach their target, the stone wall under a copse of trees. At the copse, the Federals had waiting nineteen more guns loaded with canister and grape. When the vanguard of the great charge got into their killing zone, these guns scoured and re-scoured the slope in front of the stone wall, tearing away lives and hope and Lee's purpose in his second invasion of the North.

Hood could have reversed the problem using his own guns. A modern artilleryman standing today on the gently sloping field of Franklin looking toward the old Federal lines

can imagine all the Army of Tennessee's artillery ranged behind him to volley fire into that little target of earthworks. It
is to see with lip-smacking clarity how Hood could have won
his battle: Simply hold Schofield in his trenches with surrounding infantry and drench his works with iron. That is
the artillery solution to any battle – force the other guy to
stand up for glory in a pool of his own blood and then blow
him away. But Schofield had his guns in place and Hood did
not. Hood had outrun his counter-battery weapons as he had
out-distanced his own largest corps of infantry.

For all those reasons, Hood's generals did not want to hit
the Federal position head-on. Not now, not half-prepared.
Forrest proposed leading his cavalry around the fortifications to strike Schofield from behind and cut that road up
which he had reports of Federal wagons racing pell-mell for
Nashville. Hood had proposed to Lee a similar alternative
under similar conditions on the second day of Gettysburg.
Now Hood gave Forrest the answer Lee had given him – No.
Spring Hill had made this assault "a necessity."[91] This army
had to beat the Federals in detail if it was to capture Nashville. It had to win here, now, to reinvigorate national morale
and pride with hot-blooded action, to regain the army's reputation, to reconfirm Hood's authority as commander, and
to put fighting heart back into the army for its attack on
Nashville.

Hood, furious at his hesitant generals, ordered attack
head-on in the berserker style that had won for him at
Gaines's Mill and Chickamauga and may have won Gettys-

burg on its second day if Hood leading the charge on the Union left had not been shot out of his saddle. This was a bad decision. A decision made out of anger and shame and not of any good analysis of the enemy in his concentrated, fortified position. It was a decision Hood and his army forced on each other.

Commander, generals, and army as a corporate whole had failed to preserve Atlanta. Now they risked failure in Middle Tennessee because Hood could not move his generals to move his army with the aggressive initiative needed to catch and crush half their number of inferior Yankees. They could not for many good reasons, mutual suspicion likely foremost. When his generals told Hood that Franklin was not a place to head-butt, he would not hear them for his suspicion of their motives and because they had proved to him they could not move troops with the sophistication needed for anything but direct assault. No, this battle had to be made now and entirely within the direct power of control of the general commanding. A frontal assault at Franklin was a bad decision but the only decision Hood allowed himself to make.

Still Hood's general officers protested a frontal attack, their argument fierce and some of it insubordinate. It is worth imagining these battle-burnt men looking out across another Pickett's charge toward another stone wall and already grieving for their regiments about to be thrown away. These generals knew the army must retain its capacity to move beyond this immediate battle to fight the next battle, and the battle after that, if the army were to do anything pro-

ductive for the Confederate dream. They wanted no debilitating slaughter. If the army had a numerical advantage at
this place and moment, it would have a greater advantage –
and a less costly victory – if it waited for all of the army's units
to collect on the field of battle.

They had out-marched the artillery needed to balance
those twenty-eight blue guns over there, out-marched the
heaviest infantry corps – A. P. Stewart's Third Corps – and
out-run their ammunition trains. Some troops, Forrest's
cavalry among them, were down to their last few cartridges,
and so much for Forrest's brave proposal to gallop around the
Yankee army to batter it from behind. Last, after nine days
of a brawling road race and after the morning's double-quick
time forced march from Spring Hill, the troops on hand
needed the few hours' rest granted by waiting for the remainder of the army to catch up. *Schofield, they said, is going nowhere. He is in that rat hole over there plugged by the Army of
Tennessee. General Hood can have his victory but just a bit later
today or tonight or tomorrow, and bag this blue army more cheaply
of lives with all of his combat power in his hands.*

Hood angrily overruled his generals. There is no eyewitness account of what Hood may have said to further to justify
the battle. But he believed he had a substantial local numerical superiority that guaranteed victory. Thanks to yet another failure of his intelligence team and his own poor
analysis, Hood believed Schofield's force remained scattered
across the countryside, not concentrated in those earthworks. Just go down there and knock over those broken
down old breastworks and this remnant of the Army of the

Ohio would be sent running away. "Franklin," Hood told his generals, "is the key to Nashville, and Nashville is the key to independence," and he was right.[92]

* * *

In the late afternoon of a fine Indian summer day with the air thin and brightly carrying each sound of bird and turning leaf, the sky pale blue and yellow, the trees red from green and the rolling fields stubble-brown after harvest, all smelling dusty and mellow, and over the still-continuing protests of his generals, men nearly mutinous with disbelief and outrage, Hood sent eighteen brigades – 20,000 sons, husbands, fathers – tramping across two miles of open ground, driving rabbits and quail before them, into the Federal fortifications.

These were twice as many men tramping twice as far as Pickett's terrible charge and against fortifications not softened by artillery barrage fire. Pickett failed and half of those who marched with him were killed or wounded. Perhaps it is significant that Hood had been blown out of his saddle on July 2, 1863, and lay half-conscious in a hospital tent on July 3 and was not there to see Pickett in the smoke and blood weeping for his wasted soldiers. Pickett never forgave Lee that charge.

Hood was right about one great thing and that was the thing on which he depended this day, on which all Confederate strategy depended – the furious driving power of the Southern soldier. There is a magic strength in a body of men running through enemy fire. If those men are in Confederate gray, their strength is greater still. To be in gray on that fine day and running behind those red battle flags was to be in that kind of magic.

Running across open grassland through cracking yellow and brown of artillery bursts, the buzz-past of bullets and hiss-by of iron chunks, dodging shrapnel sharp and steaming in the ground, ducking airbursts and the *whee-thunk!* of twisted metal down-driving from the sky, smell of gunpowder and sweat in the nostrils, reek of freshly upturned earth, of blood and piss and fear-made shit, running around and over and through the chopped away arms and heads and feet, the slippery eyeballs and brains and guts, the dropped hats and rifles, through the sudden sprays of blood of exploding comrades, cries and shouts and defiant yells, running around men staggering stunned and goggle-eyed, running toward the white and red flashing guns and yellow sheets of musket volley fire from the enemy earthworks, more comrades falling down falling away falling up blown to bits blown out of life snatched out of their bones and brawn by lead and trash metal, an unearthly heaping up of corpses of screaming wounded men of screaming wounded horses kicking and biting, an internal and external howl so complete it deafens, and still running terrified and unable to do anything but run and *there* they are! up ahead! the red flags! flapping and snapping and shot through! around them men in gray leaning into the lead storm as they run into grape into canister into lead bees, being torn away as they run behind the red flags, and this soldier had better run, too, and there is nothing for it but to run, to scream and to run and to shoot with no time to reload, and maybe, just maybe, to run out the other side alive!

And that is what happened. It was colossal. Hood's first assault ran over the enemy trenches and got out the other side of battle and there was a moment of stunning marvelous victory and survival. Before all the blue world caved in on that little crowd of gray heroes.

The first assault did as Hood expected. It routed that absurdly misplaced Union outpost in front of the earthworks, put there by a commander too drunk to understand his orders. But not too drunk to abandon his troops to find some safer place for himself to be. Hood's first wave ran pell-mell alongside the outpost's survivors toward the earthworks, blue and gray running so intermingled the blue riflemen in their trenches dared not shoot. Both colors overran the Federal main line and into the trenches. Then it was rifle muzzle against chest and sword and knife across throat and pistol shoved into stomach and no time for words "Yield or die!" but merely to make slaughter. Melee, medieval combat, man-on-man.

More of Hood's grays poured across the breastworks until the deliciously named Opdycke Tigers, Federal soldiers bedraggled from night-long service fighting rear guard, thinking they had earned the right to sit out this little skirmish, found themselves sprawled for rest behind the trench line over which all of Tennessee came roaring. What could these weary men do but get up and run forward, back into the maelstrom? The Tigers made a ferocious strangling, stabbing, shooting, clubbing, battering, gouging combat over the dirt and log barricades. They threw back Hood's vanguard. Major Arthur MacArthur, three times wounded and his horse shot out from under him, ran forward to drive his sword through the Confederate color bearer. Then the real fighting began.

This was killing that had no glory to it, if killing in war ever can have glory. Mutual slaughter as men on each side of the earthworks shot and slashed and clubbed each other, sometimes firing down over the wall without bothering to look. Until the outside of the barricade was so stacked with bodies that wounded men beneath were suffocated. Until the inside trench was sloshing with blood and wounded men who fell into it drowned. The Tigers fought and Schofield's blues fought and Hood's grays fought and the killing went on through the afternoon and into the night.

When that first assault was thrown back, Hood sent in more charges, as many as thirteen in some sectors, in a wild, whirling combat done piece-meal with troops pushed in as they marched up to the field. Hood made the mistake Longstreet had refused to make on July 3 at Gettysburg when Pickett's charge was shattered – Hood reinforced failure. Hood shuttled his army into the maw of a killing machine and it was eaten up. Hood, too, was wrecked.

* * *

As this Indian summer day shrank into bleak night, the ghastly combat went on. After five hours of fighting, Schofield's stubborn troops pulled the last bullets from their pockets. A soldier in torn blue, hat knocked off, face black from powder and mud and spattered with other men's blood, weighs in his gritty hand his last bullet and knows that, with one more charge, Hood has won. The soldier looks with extreme delicacy over the barricade, searching for the gray reserve that must be out there in the dark preparing to ride over these trenches and cut every blue throat, his included. But he sees fewer gray men at the wall thrusting over and stabbing through and shooting down. Fewer men in fewer organized groups. And then they are running away! hoping their bloody muddy gray will be absorbed into camouflaging night before they can be back-shot. They leave behind the dead in their pieces and the wounded in their blood. That blue soldier with his last bullet in his hand looks as deeply as he dares into the smoky whirl of a night filled with groans and shrieks of pain and resentful muzzle-flashes and he sees this part of the battle is over. Done! And he has come out alive!

There still is fighting to be done that night – skirmishers and snipers and angry vengeful men – but this Federal soldier with his last bullet in his hand has outrun the wily Hood these many days and outfought the mighty Army of Tennessee and he is too tired to cheer himself. Now comes the familiar order – *Keep silence but pull out! March like hell for Nashville! Leave the dead to bury themselves and the wounded to cure themselves. On your feet! Get onto the Nashville road and tramp north – Move out!* He marches with hot haste because that one bullet in his hand is all he will have until he sees Old Pap swinging open the gates to salvation.

Behind Schofield's fleeing regiments, the moon's shine did not penetrate the shroud of death drawn across this battlefield. Out there lay 6,252 Confederate dead and wounded, including twelve generals and fifty-three regimental colonels. Corps commander Stephen D. Lee, wounded. A division commander and five brigade commanders, killed. Two division commanders and four brigade commanders, wounded. One brigade commander, captured. Pickett lost more in less than an hour at Gettysburg. Grant at Cold Harbor lost more in eight minutes. But Franklin was the war's costliest battle in officer dead. Franklin decapitated the Army of Tennessee. Schofield, in his works and under his guns, lost 2,326.[93]

With no clear understanding of what had happened out there in the kill zone, Hood wrapped up his day with a plan to renew battle in the same style next morning. But with the sensible precaution of ordering his artillery to drive one hundred rounds per gun into the Federal works before another great assault. Meanwhile, Schofield, that good mechanical soldier, once more slunk away in the night, leaving to Hood possession of the battlefield as a false token of victory.

In a victory letter read out to his troops, Hood said, "The enemy have been sent in disorder and confusion to Nashville," and that is what the newspapers reported to Richmond. Davis cheered the rare happy news.[94]

* * *

Thomas in Nashville, working desperately to finish his defenses, had collected just 25,000 clerks, bakers, and green recruits by the day Franklin was fought. He was not ready to fight Hood's demon soldiers. He ordered Schofield to counterattack Hood across the wreckage of yesterday's battlefield.

Schofield thought that a preposterous idea. His soldiers were exhausted of strength and ammunition. For ten days now, Hood had chased and Schofield had run. Schofield had invested so much in running that now he could not bring himself to attack, bullets or not. "Why run any further risk?" this exasperated and very modern major general wrote in his memoirs.[95] Schofield marched his army into Nashville.

* * *

Franklin broke the Army of Tennessee and broke Hood and it was unnecessary. Overall, Hood's army outnumbered the rump Army of the Ohio more than two-to-one. In infantry, Hood had a three-to-two advantage and more cavalry. However, Livermore in Numbers and Losses says Hood had 22,000 "effectives" in the vicinity of Franklin and an additional 5,000 in Forrest's cavalry for a total of 27,000 on the field before his Third Corps, artillery, and auxiliaries trickled in, some arriving after the battle was over. Hood reported having put 23,000 into the combat itself. Livermore says Schofield had almost 28,000 in the vicinity of Franklin, including 6,400 cavalrymen. Schofield reported having 16,000

troops in the battle itself, the rest scattered across the countryside or pulling toward Nashville even before the battle had
begun.[96]

These numbers say that Hood had a better than two-to-
one overall advantage in the campaign, that both sides were
about equal in the immediate vicinity of Franklin, and that
Hood was right in thinking he had a substantial numerical
superiority on the battlefield itself. He had about fifty percent more troops in the fight than did Schofield. Yet, when
the battle was done, Hood had lost, and he had lost one in
four of the soldiers he had sent into the maelstrom – twenty-
seven percent. Schofield's losses were not quite fourteen percent. There is a lot to be said for good entrenchments and
twenty-eight guns.

Commanders in the mid-nineteenth century considered
that if a frontal assault as at Franklin was to win they had to
put in three times as many infantry as they faced among the
defenders. There was no military-scientific reason for this
figure but contemporaries believed it. That conclusion was
wrong but Civil War generals did not have access to modern
statistical hindsight. Hattaway and Jones in *How the North
Won* calculate that, across the entire Civil War, winning Confederate attackers outnumbered Union defenders by an average of just eight percent. In attacks lost, the Confederates
sent forward an average of just eighty-seven percent of the
defenders' numbers.[97] Hood's 23,000 striking Schofield's
16,000 were not enough by contemporary standards to win
at Franklin but they were enough by these modern statistics.
Yet Hood was beaten – by a stubborn man, stubborn works,

and twenty-eight stubborn guns. And because he had shut off every alternative means to make the battle.

Franklin was the turning point in Hood's mental state. After Atlanta, after the infuriating black comedy of Spring Hill, after so much hard-driving of this army that required hard-driving, Hood had expected an easy win at Franklin over an inferior enemy. Failure is hardest when victory is expected easily. Next morning, strapped into the saddle of a horse picking its way through torn flesh on the battlefield, through the stench of meat-rot and old gunpowder smoke, burnt wood and mud, Hood saw the face of that grim and awful creature called Failure, the beast that had crept backward from Dalton, Georgia, in Johnston's fallback campaign yowling and spitting, broken its bones and dripped its blood at Atlanta, and now, on what should have been the grand triumph of Hood's payback march, had been shorn of fur and stripped of muscle and gazed at Hood with eyes sick and dreamy, asking, *Which way now, General, to this victory of yours?*

Failure at Franklin broke Hood. The modern phrase is clinical depression but that is today's diagnosis and cannot mean much at this distance of time except very generally. Hood's condition was compounded or brought on by combat fatigue. Combat fatigue can disrupt the effectiveness of an army commander as easily as the army's rawest recruit. The term covers a collection of symptoms growing out of the cumulative effect of combat stress – the physical battering of movement across violent terrain, unrelenting fear, pent up and released and then re-suppressed aggression, the weight of command responsibility, moral fright, anxiety, dread of failure, and, most terrible of all, of self-inflicted humiliation. The soldier fears he will be proved a coward. The general fears his genius will be seen as murderous stupidity. This kind of extreme moral and physical pressure can debilitate and make useless a soldier. Sleep, rest camp, a three day pass, drugs or dope or that universal solvent of woe, alcohol, can help a soldier hold off combat fatigue for a bit and continue his or her mission. But combat fatigue is no ordinary tiredness – it is a frenzy of exhaustion.

Combat doctors studying G.I.s who fought across Normandy from the invasion beaches in World War II found that a soldier can withstand three days of intense, non-stop fighting before he must have a break or he will break.[98] Give a soldier a short rest – even so little as a hot meal in safety and a few hours' lolling on clean grass – and the soldier can endure another three days of continuous combat. But six days of heavy fighting with just an afternoon's break at midpoint is as much as an army commander can expect of front line troops before he must rotate them to rest camps. It is as much as a commander should expect of himself because a good general always is in the front line, mentally. Push a soldier beyond the six day limit – it can be done, has been done, is done – and he will fail. He will fail to fight or he will make a mistake and die or he will breakdown mentally or he may go berserk.

After Hood's bloody failure to save Atlanta, after his odd behavior in Alabama hiding out from Beauregard, after the comedy of Spring Hill, after the frustration and exhaustion of a nine days' fighting road race with Schofield through

Middle Tennessee, Hood showed too many of the classic symptoms of combat fatigue – restlessness, irritability, decreased efficiency, deviation from normal temperament.[99] After Franklin, Hood displayed much of the full blown last symptoms – demoralization and reduced or lost power of decision.[100] To look at the weeks after Franklin is to see Hood so frenzied with exhaustion that he is almost an automaton marching men into an environment so dangerous it requires the absolute alertness and concentration that Hood no longer has.

There is for a commander one great, if temporary, cure for combat fatigue and that is to create a victory.[101] Victory grants release from fatigue. As Hood marched his army out of Franklin's blood and into Nashville's winter sleet, he was a broken man, no longer competent to keep his command. But all that could change if he could fashion a victory at Nashville. That hope, that hunger, that need took Hood into his last battle.

* * *

Hood had lost the initiative. He had decapitated his own army. He had cost himself a vast number of front-line troop casualties. He had to know that, with Schofield's riflemen now inside Nashville, the city garrison was at least equal in numbers to his own depleted army. Hood's victory message to Richmond, sent on December 3 and received eleven days later on the eve of the Battle of Nashville, reported none of this.

Hood likely thought a triumph at Nashville would obliterate the disaster of the victory he had proclaimed at Franklin. But Hood no longer had the strength to capture the city and its vast military stores. No strength to threaten the Ohio Valley to lure Grant away from Richmond and Lee. The Army of Tennessee no longer had war-winning potential. Hood no longer was a great captain. To see Hood in eyewitness accounts of this moment is to see a man doing the commander's job empty of drive or inspiration but unwilling to quit.

Yet a wounded Hood and a wounded Army of Tennessee remained a grim power glaring into the face of Grant's continental plan and what they did at Nashville proved their capacity. Hood had five options to consider and he had to have thought about them all. First, he could barrel into Nashville as his campaign plan had promised Beauregard and Davis. Second, retreat to Alabama to rebuild the army to prepare to try something else. Third, bypass Nashville and raid into Kentucky, a potentially fruitful option. Fourth, strike any large target of opportunity elsewhere in Tennessee where he might win. Any kind of win would be a boost to army and Southern morale. Fifth, fortify himself outside Nashville and taunt Thomas to come out to fight and then shatter the Rock of Chickamauga.

The first option was the hot-blooded choice, the newspaper and popular choice, but it was out of Hood's reach. The army no longer had the strength to attack Nashville and expect to win. The gray against blue troop numbers were insufficient and not even the customary hell-raising power of the Confederate soldier could overcome them.

The second option, retreat to Alabama, would cost Hood his command as surely as it had Johnston falling back on Atlanta – Davis rewarded retreating generals with dismissal and humiliation. Retreat would waste Hood's sacrifice of Georgia to Sherman. It would isolate Hood between Sherman and the Union-held Mississippi River. It risked massive desertions as despondent Tennessee soldiers found themselves marching away from homes they had come to save from Yankee depredation. The army could dissolve. Retreat also would cost Hood any hope of reshaping his newspaper reputation. At this point in the war, it probably was worth Hood's life to avoid battle at Nashville. Rabid Confederates were lynching defeatists across the South. Retreat from Nashville would look like defeatism to the fever-eyed, last-ditchers in a Southern population radicalized by disaster and stunned to discover that Grant's blue soldiers would not be stopped.

The third option – bypassing Nashville for Kentucky – risked having Thomas fall on Hood from behind. Half the reason Lee fought Gettysburg was fear of turning his back on George Meade, a man not just hungry for a fight but expected by his government and people to make the biggest brawl he could find. Neither Hood nor Beauregard had provided the Army of Tennessee with the logistical strength needed to bypass Nashville. Supply to this campaign was predicated on Hood's getting into Nashville's warehouses to equip the army for Hood's next big move, into the Ohio Valley or on to Richmond.

The fourth option, hitting a lesser but more achievable target of opportunity somewhere else in Tennessee, seemed a good bet, at least to Beauregard. "From Franklin," Beauregard later argued, "General Hood should have marched not to Nashville, but on Murfreesboro, which could doubtless have been captured[,]...destroyed the railroad bridges...[and so] caused the evacuation of Bridgeport and Chattanooga..."[102] Yes, but does that win the war and just how quickly would Grant solve the problem?

None of these four options offered Hood any real chance to stage his heroic march on Richmond to liberate Lee and that is why he took up the fifth option. Hood chose to fortify himself outside Nashville and to tease Old Pap into coming out to fight on ground of Hood's choosing. The classic Lee invitation to battle. It also was the best Hood could do with battered, hungry men with bleeding feet and winter howling down upon them. The best that could be done by a general too poorly supported by an exhausted national government and inflexible national strategy to have any alternative.

In his memoirs, Hood justified his decision writing that he marched on to Nashville for the sake of his soldiers' pride and for Southern pride. One more great fight, even a failure, was too important to the South to forego. As with the old political war against abolition, the South had to continue to resist everywhere and at all times.

Hood arrived outside Nashville with his heaviest infantry corps – barely used in the last hours of Franklin – and his artillery fat with the ammunition not fired at Franklin. Spies and townsmen told him Thomas's main force was raw and weak and the stiffening provided by Schofield's veteran troops was thin because Hood had chased those men into exhaustion. *Now is the moment to trample the barricades and free the city,* they said to Hood, *all the Confederate townsmen will rise up to help.* That promise must have sounded sweet to Hood but he knew he was unable comply. He could only wait to be attacked.

Hood entrenched his army – doing what he despised for the heart he believed it took out of his soldiers – and fortified heavily. He built a fallback line two miles behind his frontline and fortified that. He stretched his army across all the roads leading south out of Nashville, demarking a new come-and-get-me boundary of the Confederacy. He sent his cavalry under Forrest galloping across the state to keep reinforcements away from Thomas and to cut telegraph and rail lines into the city. He was preparing to the best of his flagging abilities for the greatest battle of his career.

Because an army on the march consumes greatly and wastes greatly, Hood was short on food, shoes, and blankets. His soldiers shivered and hungered in their entrenchments. But Hood had plenty of ammunition and his troops remained tough, zealous, and invigorated on their native soil. He believed Nashville was his if Thomas would come out to fight before the gray army's resources were eaten up and winter froze hands to guns.

* * *

Breaking the Unbreakable

Hood entrenched his remaining 23,000 infantry and artillery, and perhaps 5,000 of cavalry, in front of the most heavily fortified city on the continent – after Richmond and Washington – and waited for Thomas to be taunted into Hood-like rashness to run out of his barricades to fight.

Across the battle line, George Thomas looked over his earthworks at the curling smoke of his enemy's campfires, seeming to stretch from horizon to horizon below the city, and thought only a fool like Hood would assault this fortress-city and only a fool like Hood could take it. Thomas felt in his coat pocket the heat of the latest telegram from another kind of furious war-maker. *Attack him!* wrote Grant, *Hit him now while he's disorganized and vulnerable, hit him hard, smash him up! Knock him away from the Ohio so I can continue to heap the pressure on Lee without any more Western distraction!*

Hood begged Thomas to fight and Grant ordered him to attack but Thomas would not. Not until the moment was ripe, with the last button buttoned on a soldier's tunic, the last bullet counted into a soldier's hand, the last pencil mark made on a battle map, the last nail hammered into the last horseshoe. Until then, Thomas would use an Armada strategy – he would wait for Nashville winter to shrivel his enemy before Thomas had to fight him.

Thomas was given Nashville because Sherman knew that to put Thomas there was to transport the Rock from Chickamauga onto Hood's highway north. Thomas was never driven from any battlefield on which he fought. He was Virginia-born and too much a Southern man to quit any fight. At Chickamauga, with the Federal army breaking apart around him and Longstreet's divisions stampeding uphill to blow apart his own corps, his men down to their last three bullets apiece, Thomas gave the order, "Fix bayonets and go for them!"[103] In that stubborn moment, he became the Rock. Nor, Grant must have thought in his growing impatience, was stubborn Thomas ever driven to a battlefield.

Thomas did not immediately strike as Hood arrived outside Nashville because Thomas saw the odds against him. Despite Schofield's boasting and the meager facts Thomas had scrounged, Thomas had no real idea what kind of damage Schofield had inflicted on Hood at Franklin. Thomas knew he faced a wild general and a hot army and thought himself heavily out-matched in numbers – perhaps two-to-one – and certainly outmatched in the fighting quality of troops.

Too few of Thomas's re-enlisted veterans had yet returned to him from their election districts. He had lost another 15,000 veterans at the expiration of their terms of service. In exchange, Thomas got 12,000 recruits, making for a dumbing-down of his total combat force and a loss of sturdiness on the firing line. He had gained Schofield's now 19,500 effectives but they were played out. The preening, rivalrous Schofield was himself another problem. Thomas had some veteran cavalry but they still were finding mounts and saddles. Thomas had at his call 75,000 troops strung across Tennessee on sentry duty but too few could be risked away from their posts with Forrest galloping through the state.[104] Then, on December 1, like an early Christmas gift and as Hood's lead elements came in sight of the city, nearly 20,000 troops from Missouri under Major General Andrew Jackson Smith tied up at Nashville's wharf. Now Thomas had his fighting numbers.

* * *

A freezing rain blew in and struck for six days, giving Thomas his Armada weather. Through his binoculars, Thomas could see Hood's troops driving spades into frozen ground and shivering over campfires. His scouts and cavalry reported too many of these gray men were hungry, wrapping bare feet in bundles of rag, wearing blankets for uniforms. Thomas saw that, even if his good new numbers made the moment ripe for attack, he should continue to wait for General Winter to freeze the soldiers of the Army of Tennessee into shatterable figures.

His problem was Grant. For Grant's continental plan, Thomas had to wreck Hood now so that Grant could know the South's only army still free to maneuver was wiped out of the equation of war and that Grant had nothing more on which to concentrate but Lee. More than that, Grant had in him a hunger to kill the Army of Tennessee because he saw it could be killed. After four awful years of war, the Northern armies and Northern people deserved a great killing spectacle in the West. Each day that Thomas delayed was a day's grace for the Army of Tennessee, gifting it time to recover and dig deeper. Another day in which Hood, the general of whom nothing could be expected but the unexpected, could contrive to avoid the killing blow. To outflank Thomas, get into the Ohio Valley, and snap the fragile threads by which Grant so carefully was pulling the war toward Northern victory.

* * *

Out there, across no man's land, Hood also sought to gather in reinforcements. He looked west, but Richard Taylor, with 33,000 troops garrisoned across Alabama, Mississippi, and east Louisiana, and in his wonderful arrogance, refused. Hood called into Missouri for troops and was refused. Hood expected swarms of Tennessee volunteers and got just 164 while 254 veteran cavalrymen deserted from one division alone. He tried to conscript Tennessee men and to impress labor to repair his rail line of supply but the civilian population fled away from its army.[105] Davis told him to drag back absentees but by now nearly 200,000 men had deserted all Confederate armies and how was Hood to make war on deserters when he had Thomas to fight? Too many shoeless soldiers left bloody trails in the ice. Hood was exhausted by depression and work. He was no more the dashing golden boy. He distracted himself by taking political revenge on Major General Cheatham for the Spring Hill comedy, sabotaging the man's reputation and career. Then Hood relented and wrote the War Department a recantation. He brooded. The army's morale sagged. Soldiers began to sing derisive songs about their commander.

* * *

A new and more ghastly ice storm blew in on December 9 and stuck over the city and the bleak hills in which huddled the Army of Tennessee. The storm persisted four wretched days. From the warmth of Nashville, Thomas wrote Washington that "the whole country is now covered with a sheet of ice so hard and slippery it is utterly impossible for troops to ascend the slopes, or even to move over level ground in anything like order."[106] Cavalry horses fell on their riders. Gun carriage wheels broke through the ice crust and the artillery could not be shoved or dragged.

Hood, shivering in his fortifications, on December 3 sent Richmond a one-paragraph report on his victory at Franklin.[107] The message was received on December 14. Richmond already had heard rumors of a horror out West. While the Army of Tennessee shrank and the enemy grew, Forrest's 5,000 cavalry whooping through Tennessee and Kentucky were so cut up by blue commanders with a new Grant-like hardness in them that they were lost to Hood in his final battle.

Beneath the lashings of the ice storm and of Washington, Thomas continued his methodical preparations. On December 6, Grant cabled: "Attack Hood at once..." Thomas would not. On December 8, Grant cabled: "Now is one of the finest opportunities ever presented of destroying one of the three armies of the enemy. If destroyed, he can never replace it." Thomas did not budge. Grant, in exasperation, wrote Halleck: "There is no better man to repel an attack than Thomas but I fear he is too cautious to ever take the initiative." A sarcastic Secretary of War, Edwin Stanton, wrote Grant: "Thomas seems unwilling to attack because it is hazardous, as if all war was anything but hazardous."[108]

Lincoln, Grant, Stanton, and Halleck were men of nightmarish apprehensions – the blood of 300,000 Union dead and wounded and the national treasure draining away at five million dollars a day inflicted them with horror of failure. For abolitionist Lincoln, slavery was finished in the North and all conquered territory. But a shattered United States could not enforce abolition across the continent. The war had to be won and the nation reunited for slavery to be destroyed utterly. Now, coming up through Tennessee, was an eccentric and dynamic general driving on a great, aggressive army to shatter the North's growing hope of victory.

Lincoln, Grant, Stanton, and Halleck knew no more than did Jefferson Davis, or George Thomas, just how much damage Schofield had inflicted at Franklin. Their reports of the battle were incomplete. Schofield's braggardly tales had to be discounted. What they did know was that out there shivering in the cold and yearning for a chair by a fireplace in

Nashville was a berserker chieftain who would fight when he had the tools and fight when he had no tools at all. Lincoln must have looked at Hood and yearned to have had a dozen of him in the Union armies in the bitter first years of the war. *A dozen Hoods in blue with Grant in command and the war would have been done long ago!*

By unhappy contrast, they saw inside Nashville a man – George Thomas – so concentrated on finding horseshoes and stacking up repeating rifles that he was about to miss the main chance. He would let Hood get past him into the grain-producing heartland of the Old Northwest. Lincoln, Grant, and Halleck surely must have regretted letting Sherman swagger through Georgia with his 62,000 good old boys instead of killing the Army of Tennessee with its wild commander. Something had to be done at Nashville. If Thomas would not attack this day, then Grant had to shift the command to someone who would.

Grant prepared to give the command to Schofield.[109] Schofield very much wanted the honor and glory of the hour he saw coming. He was chafing to bash into the old West Point roommate who had hounded him through Middle Tennessee. Schofield was the one man who could see clearly that Hood was finished. He also saw that the glory would go not to the general who won Franklin but to the general who inflicted the *coup de grace* at Nashville.

At last, an exasperated Grant cabled Halleck to relieve Thomas on December 9 and give the command to Schofield.[110] Lincoln was stunned to watch Grant remove the hero of Chickamauga but did not interfere. Halleck persuaded Grant to delay the order in hopes that Thomas would attack. Finally, on December 13, Thomas understood he was to be relieved of his command.[111] To be sure, Halleck wrote Thomas on December 14 this critical sentence holding open the possibility of a suspension of the order: "Every day's delay on your part...seriously interferes with General Grant's plans." Those five blue arrows.[112]

There followed a scene at Thomas's headquarters not have been much different from that played out a few months earlier in the headquarters of the Army of Tennessee when Hood took command from Johnston but with a radically different and telling outcome.[113] There are no secrets in an army about the rise and fall of its commanding general. Orders that cannot pass Confederate raiders cutting telegraph wires or heavy ice tearing down the lines mysteriously appear in army gossip. Thomas's subordinate commanders knew of Grant's intent to relieve Thomas. They knew Thomas had resisted the first order by telegraphing Halleck and Grant with promises to attack when the ice storm lifted. They knew, as Thomas had just learned, that Schofield was playing the Hood role in sending Grant messages undercutting Thomas. Schofield thought Thomas an incompetent and a sluggard and believed himself the true hero of the hour. He saw at last his moment of glory arriving when Grant would give him this command.

But the assembled general officers were flabbergasted at Grant's relief order. Did the general-in-chief commanding all United States land forces mean to change horses in mid-stream, with the enemy a cannon-shot away, when so much was prepared for the attack and only the weather held them back? When that enemy out there was ferocious and unpredictable and, no matter what Schofield claimed for Franklin, never an enemy to underestimate? When each of these blue generals was chomping at the bit to get out there and smash Hood, tear down his traitor's banners, unseat his guns, rip apart his regiments, and send his soldiers weeping back to Alabama?

Imagine Schofield standing there listening to all this and coming to realize, with a sickening slowness or perhaps a lightning pang, that he was not going to get the command after all. That these angry men, their professionalism – no, their patriotism! – impugned by Grant's outrageous decree would talk Thomas into ignoring the order. That is what they did: *I obey*, said the viceroy of the Philippines to the King of Spain, *but do not comply*. And then Schofield, too, had to concur. The man who believed he already had won the fight would not have the glory he had earned. They all – all – agreed Thomas would hold Grant's order until the weather cleared and they would attack and do the job they had to do. Then let Grant come to Nashville and lop off heads if they lost the battle. That is what they said and they were bold about it, as bold as veterans of that war had a right to be.

But this was Grant they were talking about. Grant, who waged war on the horrific and bloody Biblical scale, the nation's warlord of warlords, who had at his command more combat power than ever before had been assembled in this hemisphere and, with repeating rifles and other modern weapons at its disposal, outclassed any army ever before seen on the planet. To look at his photograph, Grant does not appear an impatient man. But he was. As impatient as any commander must be who has been given the responsibility of saving his nation. Impatient to win the war, to end the killing.

Knowing that about Grant makes it easier to imagine what those men standing there in that room watching Thomas fold the order into his pocket must have thought Grant would do to each of them if they failed to whip Hood. They must have been, in a measure appropriate to each, afraid. Grant was not a man to kick ass and take names. No, he would do worse, far worse. He would exact the most terrible price. Fail now, disobey this order and fail to win the battle, and Grant's rebuke would mean a lifetime of dishonor for each man in this room, scorn at home, the wonder and shame of wives and children, and of children beyond those children. Shame to the last generations of their names. To these men who conspired in committee to circumvent the orders of U.S. Grant, General-in-Chief, Commanding, that had to have been their most profound incentive to win this fight.

Thomas's assembled commanders thought a few moments further and suddenly decided that logistics and the weather and the moment had arrived. They told Thomas to attack. Thomas telegraphed Halleck, "The ice having melted away to-day, the enemy will be attacked to-morrow morning."[114]

Unknown to the men in that room, at that moment Grant, impatient and angry, was making his way toward Union Station in Washington City for his train to Nashville. He was going West. He was going to lop heads. He was going to make things happen himself.[115] And he was furious to be diverted from strangling the life out of Lee.

* * *

THE END AT NASHVILLE

A warm rain thawed the ice and turned the planet, so far as the eye could see, to mud. Thomas called for reveille at 4:00 A.M. the next day, December 15. D-day. H-hour.

The Rock had assembled nearly 50,000 troops to send out against Hood's 23,000 infantry and artillery and whatever few of cavalry Forrest had not taken away to waste.[116] Thomas needed that many more not just because he was attacking over open ground into heavy fortifications but because his soldiers overall were no match for Hood's. Thomas interspersed veterans with the inexperienced. If too much of his human material was poor, he had plenty of the world's best war *materiél*. Thomas armed his cavalry and as many infantry as he could with seven-shot Spencer repeating rifles and carbines so that a single bluebelly cook could put as much lead into the air as a half dozen grayback veterans. Schofield's Hood-hardened troops, rested and refitted, were the key to Thomas's combat plan – they would be his battle-winning shock force.

In the murk of pre-dawn, blue soldiers threw off their blankets to peer out of their fortifications into a fog that clung to the ice-chipped mud. They were as anxious, frightened, ready, and unready as any troops ever have been. The battle-opening artillery fire did their nerves no good. The banging guns were fog-muffled and not heroic, their muzzle flashes subdued, the overhead sizzle of the shells unearthly weird in the cloud-thickened atmosphere. Nothing like the bright spark of Fourth of July that these men, in their dirt, sweat, mud, and fear, needed to boost them across all that open ground into the rifle muzzles of Hell's minions.

When they finally were mustered from behind the city walls into no man's land, they found the air there filling up with flying metal. They could not see their enemy or his works through the smoke and fog. But they were commanded to march. They marched. They were freezing and steaming together, dripping the sweat of fright and the wetness of the fog cloud. Their weapons misted over. About 7:00 A.M. their left wing – the First Brigade of U.S. Colored Troops, all the men former slaves[117] – had the happy unhappy honor to take and give the first face-to-face fire with the Army of Tennessee. The great fight began. Incredibly, or perhaps not considering Hood's mental state, and despite nearly two weeks of the interplay of spies and analysis of intelligence, Thomas had caught Hood by surprise. By surprise!

Fog, like a theater curtain pulled up, lifted from between the two armies and Old Pap attacked through a bright new day. He charged on Grant's continental strategy. With the tactics of a man who knows too many of his troops are too raw for sophisticated maneuver. Thomas struck all along the Confederate battle line at once, pinning down Hood's units so they could not reinforce weak spots. He heavily assaulted both flanks. He sent cavalry galloping around the Confederate left. He put courage into his troops with close-support artillery fire, the guns dragged through the mud to pour hot metal into the gray fortress. By mid-afternoon, his lead infantrymen were firing through the embrasures of Hood's works. The Rock had moved and would not move again until Hood's line buckled, broke, and was destroyed.

At 4:00 P.M., Thomas ordered the charge of his shock troops. Schofield attacked. Blue men all along the line cheered and ran forward. They drove gray men out of their works and sent them running south, running for their lives. Winter's early night closed in. Fighting ceased. Thomas ordered his exultant cooks and bakers and his veterans to recharge their weapons and sleep with them on the cold battlefield. *Be ready*, he said, *for whatever comes next*. But he need tell them nothing. His men had the scent of victory in their nostrils. They were happy to shiver in the mud not to lose the great and prideful victory they had won and the honor and adventure that was coming to them tomorrow. *Whenever before had cooks and bakers and goggling recruits*, they said to each other, *with a smattering of veterans, won such a colossal battle?* They would sleep in the cold mud for the pleasure of keeping claim to the battlefield they had won.

But Thomas did not expect more battle. He had thrown back the Confederates with such heavy losses he assumed Hood would use the night to creep away toward Alabama. There would be fighting the next day, yes, but no more battle. Any sensible commander could see that. But that was Hood over there across the frontline. Hood did not withdraw, and now Thomas was surprised.

Hood in the night moved back two miles to his fallback entrenchments and there he waited, the wounded Moloch. Once more he had redrawn the boundary of the Confederacy, this time closer to failure. There is little direct evidence of what Hood himself did that night or of his state of mind. Was he Caesar kicking among his tired men to threaten and cheer them on, to attend himself to every detail of preparation, to make sure the battle flag was up, the trumpeter ready, the arrows fledged, the swords well-edged? Was he Henry V in gloomy disguise debating with his soldiers a king's responsibility for so much slaughter and seeking the key to inspire his army? Or was he worn down to the nub of the question, *Have I failed and is nothing more left to me but to fight?* If Hood's cut up, ragged, half-beaten army had just one more day of fight left in it, then Hood, who was Hood, would fight until he and his army were blown to pieces. He would not leave this place without one last battle, one last long grab for victory and a Confederate future.

Thomas did not want another combat and did not have to
make one. He looked across the awful, flesh-strewn battlefield and was content – if that word can be used of such a
scene – to let the remnant Army of Tennessee wither away to
zero in the foul weather. Let them stay in their fallback
trenches and barricades and freeze to ice men. They could
not leave this place without fear of Thomas attacking them
in rear. Federal cavalry would assure they got no supplies or
reinforcements, if the mock-Confederacy had any to send.
Thomas could bombard them at a distance, if he pleased, and
the hot iron cracking overhead would be all the warmth they
would have on that dreadful plain. Why risk a fair victory already won for the hope of a grand victory, especially when the
army out there was Hood's and Thomas's own just a two-
week collection of men?

But Thomas's commanders wanted more war. *More victory! More smash 'em up! We have this gray army at knife's point,
let's kill it!* Schofield was chief among those demanding another assault because he saw his own troops leading the great
work that could snatch back for him the glory of Franklin.
They all thought of Grant.

Once more Thomas accepted the vote of the committee of
generals. Once more he struck all along the Confederate line.
Once more The Rock had moved. Once more the Army of
Tennessee fought with desperate ferocity – 3,000 Federals
were killed in these two days of battle – and held back
Thomas's outnumbering, hodgepodge force for most of the
second day of battle. In this last day of its fighting life, the
great Army of Tennessee proved itself stubbornly heroic. Its

cause was unfit, its dream rotten, its commander adrift in lost fantasy, but its soldiers were great fighting men.

If Hood's engineers had planted his second fighting line better, he may have held off Thomas and dragged the battle into a third day to claim a draw. But, when Old Pap, with the shade of a bloody-eyed Grant at his shoulder, saw the moment right, he sent in Schofield and his veterans with the laconic words, "You may attack, General."[118] Schofield's troops ran forward yelling their battle cries, like great abolitionist crusaders on the roll to save the Union and break slavery. The Army of Tennessee bent, split, and shattered.

No time to repair broken regiments. No rallying of scattered troops. No chance to load and fire. Gray men ran, a despairing rabble. Federals climbed cheering over the captured works, waving their striped flags in victory frenzy as Confederates pelted south into the cover of the trees and churning night. It was over. The end. The Army of Tennessee had ceased to be. The war in the West was finished.

* * *

Grant got the news of the first day's victory on December 15, 1864, while on his train to Nashville. He cabled Thomas, "Push the enemy now, and give him no rest until he is entirely destroyed."[119] Grant stopped his journey and returned to the Army of the Potomac. He seems never to have forgiven Thomas for the misery Thomas put him through in the first half of that December.

* * *

Beauregard and Confederate Secretary of War Seddon got the news in a message from Hood sent on December 17 during the Army's scramble out of Tennessee. It was a single paragraph shocking for what little it said and the great deal it did not say. Richmond got more news from startling tales carried out of the West and from Northern newspapers.[120]

* * *

Over the next thirteen days, in the greatest cavalry pursuit of the war, across muddy roads, through swollen, icy streams, beneath "rain, rain, rain," sleet and snow, the Federals hounded Hood and his army's wreckage out of Tennessee.[121] The blue cavalry rode in the good Jominian fashion taught at West Point – "If beaten, the enemy must be pursued relentlessly." Forrest's gray cavalry tried to hold them off, salvaging what it could of blankets, wagons, ammunition as the wreckage of an army dragged itself southward.[122] A retreating Confederate wrote home that he had seen Hood in his tent "pulling his hair with one hand...and crying as though his heart would break."[123]

* * *

Of the 50,000 soldiers Hood had taken into Tennessee five weeks earlier, he brought just 18,000 ragged men to rest camps and hospitals in Alabama and Mississippi. He had lost over fifty percent of the army's combat troops – 8,600 as casualties, 13,200 as prisoners of war, 2,000 as deserters. He had lost nearly all of the army's artillery. He had no wagons or draft animals, no food, no winter clothing, few blankets. "The whole army," one of Hood's officers wrote, "cannot muster 5,000 effective men. Great numbers are going home every day, many never more to return, I fear. Nine-tenths of the men and line officers are bare footed and naked."[124]

Hood had delayed reporting Franklin to Richmond and now he did not report Nashville. But appalling rumors of what had happened came to the Confederate capital from the West. By Christmas Day, the story of Nashville combined with Sherman's capture of Savannah at the end of his March to the Sea on December 21 "filled the land with gloom."[125] In his first official communication with higher headquarters since December 11, Hood telegraphed this bizarrely dishonest message to Beauregard on January 3, 1865: "The army has recrossed the Tennessee River, without material loss since the battle in front of Nashville. It will be assembled in a few days in the vicinity of Tupelo, to be supplied with shoes and clothing, and to obtain forage for the animals."[126] Beauregard must have read this dispatch in puzzled anger. So much had depended on Hood's campaign. Beauregard had let it go forward, could not have stopped it. Now all was wasted. The campaign, the army, the opportunity, all gone. *And Hood sends me this quibbling message?*

Beauregard made his way to the army across the ruin of the Southern railways to see for himself what had happened.

In his pocket he had Davis's authority to fire Hood and replace him with Richard Taylor if Beauregard judged it meet
to make the swap. Taylor was an unspectacular general of
whom no romantic dash could be expected. But he was a
sound man and all that was available.

Hood's depression, despair, and disconnect from reality
did not prevent his seeing Beauregard as the demon of failure working across the ruined Southland to shore up political
support for yet another presidential decision to sack another
commander of the Army of Tennessee. Now, at last, the truth
of the Middle Tennessee campaign would come out – the true
casualty lists, Hood's fantasy journey back toward Lee, the
ghastly error of the president's personal choice of placing in
command at the Confederacy's last desperate moment a general unsuited to the challenge. Two days before Beauregard
arrived at army headquarters, Hood cabled Confederate Secretary of War James Seddon to "request to be relieved from
the command of this Army."[127]

* * *

January 15, 1865 – Beauregard arrives at the army's base at
Tupelo, Mississippi, and is stunned by what he sees. "If not,
in the strict sense of the word, a disorganized mob, it was no
longer an army." At the order of the Secretary of War,
Beauregard accepts Hood's resignation. The army has been
starved into banditry. Beauregard orders it disarmed to end
"depredations daily committed...by soldiers with arms in
their hands."[128]

January 16 – Hood changes his mind and cables Davis seeking to preserve his command.[129]

January 16 – The Confederate Congress requests Davis reappoint Joe Johnston to command of the remnant Army of Tennessee.

January 17 – Beauregard relieves Hood and appoints Richard Taylor to command.

January 19 – Taylor arrives at Tupelo and takes over an army that he and Beauregard consider ruined beyond "further hope and endurance."[130]

January 23 – Hood leaves the army, cabling his president that "I wish to cross the Mississippi River to bring to your aid 25,000 troops. I know this can be accomplished, and earnestly desire this chance to do you so much good service. Will explain my plan on arrival. I leave to-day for Richmond."[131] What Davis, confronted with the collapsing Confederate dream, may think of this newest fantasy is not recorded.

With the Army of Tennessee blasted away and no more hope of its saving the Army of Northern Virginia at Richmond, a last-minute effort by European financiers to reorganize Confederate credit to resupply the war through a new fleet of fast blockade-runners collapses.[132] The national treasury is bankrupt. The victory promised by Hood had been the government's last hope to find money to continue the war.

So, too, collapses the mood of the South. No fervid newsprint-patriotism or vigilante action can re-inflame this lost hope. The bloody-minded firebrands and cynical slave-owning aristocrats who made a rebellion against the United

States now howl in their losing frenzy for a rebellion against the government they had created, crying out for an "internal revolution" that will reform everything and win the war.[133] *Make the great Lee dictator!* Then require him to pull out of the smoking hulk of the Confederate dream some strange wonder to unbalance the planet, free the South, and preserve the moneymaking machine of slavery.

Across the combat frontier, Grant looks at his continental battle map and sees he has just one more blue arrow to drive home for victory – the arrow through the heart of the Army of Northern Virginia. That will be the final lancing of the pustule of slavery and secession. It will open a reordering of the commonwealth for a sweeter American Dream.

Fresh from his happy rampage through Georgia and South Carolina, Sherman steers his great army of bummers toward Richmond to add weight to the final blue arrow.

Beauregard sends 15,000 men – the last of the Army of Tennessee – into Georgia to catch Sherman. But the farther this unhappy remnant marches from its home state, the faster it melts away in desertions home.

* * *

Hood traveled to Richmond to make his official report. The last hope of the South was now a stunned failure from whom a heroic dream had been ripped. Only in Richmond would he know what more he had lost – reputation, rank, pride, friendship, and the girl.

Hood rocked along battered rails in a peeling carriage, across torn up roads, through burnt villages, along ravaged fields, seeing white and black women and children staggering lost in a devastated world, acres of the buried honored dead, forests shot away by cannon fire, plantations and factories gutted, rivers polluted with corpses, survivors made hysterical by vigilantes, bandits, hunger. Too few still-defiant flags tacked to flagpoles. In Richmond, within the hearing of the great testifier and gossip Mary Chesnut, the ruined man "said he had nobody to blame but himself" for the Middle Tennessee disaster.[134] But Hood's after-action report began with stranger and truer words: "The results of a campaign," he wrote, "do not always show how the General in command has discharged his duties."[135]

He had, Hood reported, done a thorough commanding general's job. But somehow the campaign had gone astray. Or perhaps not somehow but because of the failures of his corps commanders, those unmovable men. Of his generals of division at Spring Hill, Cheatham and dead Cleburne foremost. Of his regimental colonels at Franklin, so many of them too easily killed. Of his soldiers at Nashville who would not rally after they were beaten a second time in two days. His mistake, he told an Alabama newsman, "had not been in planning or making the campaign but in overestimating the valor of the troops."[136]

Hood's report was both right and wrong. The army had failed its general and the general had failed his army. The Confederate government had failed them both. The Middle Tennessee campaign – apart from Hood's rescue fantasy –

was a good plan but Hood was not the commander to make it a success. He should not have been given the job by Davis. Hood's subordinate generals were inexperienced at corps management and maneuver and confused by Hood's command style. They did not do their jobs well but they were Davis men. The traditional coin of Confederate victories – that stalwart man in gray with his rifle – was not enough to save the campaign from all these mistakes. Not when the soldier was poorly supported by a Confederate military and political leadership that no longer had any idea how to win its war.

* * *

In late winter and early spring of 1865, Hood wandered Virginia and South Carolina, seeking friends and solace. He was turned away. Too many of those who had lionized him in his days of success now despised him for what he had cost them – their personal faith in Southern victory. "Gen. Hood is here, on crutches, attracting no attention."[137] Men whose military promotions Hood had arranged, whose political power he strengthened, whose marriage proposals he championed forgot his name, except to counsel Buck Preston and her father to refuse him. Around February 5, two weeks after Hood left the army he had wrecked, Buckie broke off their engagement.

By April, Hood claimed to those who would hear him that he had been offered a command in West Virginia but that he would go to Texas, instead, where his climb to military glory had begun, to raise new gray armies. Hood went west, part of that crowd sidling toward Texas so that "when the hanging starts" they could slip across into Mexico.[138] These were the demagogues and slave-men who had stashed their fortunes in Europe and now wanted to join their money in safety. The firebrands, war criminals, and war profiteers skipping out to leave the poor and unprepared of the South to deal with Yankee victory and retribution. These were the twice-made traitors – they had betrayed the United States and now betrayed their fellow Southerners by leaving them unsuccored in the starving ruins of the Confederacy. Hood was not of their kind but he drifted west with them because the West is where ruined Americans go to find healing.

* * *

if i cood git home ide tri dam hard to git thare. my old horse is plaid out or ide trie to go now. maibee ile start to nite fur ime dam tired uv this war fur nuthin.

– Letter from a Confederate soldier[139]

After Nashville the Confederate hope was gone except in the most fanatic of Southern breasts. The Confederate revolution began to unwind faster and faster. Common soldiers crept away from their buddies and their torn battle flags for the higher cause of going home to care for starving families. On the first day of 1865, 198,000 Confederate soldiers were absent without leave.[140] Active Confederate forces scattered across half the continent, living hand to mouth, numbered

100,000 against the 400,000 troops the North had put on Southern soil, with thousands more ready to march south.[141] "Generals are as plentiful as blackberries," said Mary Chesnut, "but they have no one to command."[142] The Confederate dollar was worth two United States cents. The Confederate government called on Southern women to shear their long hair for sale in Europe to raise money to fill blockade-runners with military supplies. Despite censorship and vigilantism, people dared to say aloud the war was lost.

Radicals shouting for a dictatorship by Lee dreamed that a Union overconfident of victory would have "difficulty in replenishing the Federal armies" such that "Gen. Lee may be able to make another grand campaign" to drive the North to "inaugurate real negotiations."[143] *If that fails, we hold out until the next U.S. presidential election – 1868 – when our continued stubborn resistance must persuade the North to give up and go away.*

But the Southern people had been deluded into war in 1861 and could not be deluded into continuing the war in 1865. Despite press censorship, they knew their country was wrecked and would have no relief from anywhere. That the radicals and slaver elite that had brought them to this wretched condition would fight to the death of the last ordinary man, woman, and child and then flee to their fortunes stored in London or Cuba. They knew that in this war about elections Northerners had voted to destroy the South for its crime of making this great civil war.

In his despair, Davis took to his bed with another illness and suspended his newest fantasy – an offer to abolish slavery in return for European armies. Instead, he proposed arming slaves in exchange for the emancipation of black veterans and their families: "Let us say to every negro who wishes to go into the ranks on condition of being free – 'Go and fight; you are free'!"[144] Lee lobbied for the legislation. He wanted more soldiers for his army. The Confederate congress was stunned at this bizarre renunciation of the war's purpose. "If slaves will make good soldiers," said Georgia fire-eater Howell Cobb, "our whole theory of slavery is wrong."[145] In the North, liberated slaves and free blacks did make good soldiers – by war's end, twelve percent of all U.S. soldiers and sailors were black men[146] – and that was evident to some fighting men in gray. In February, 1864, Major General Patrick Cleburne, an Irish division commander in the Army of Tennessee, prepared a generals' petition calling for freedom for slaves who would fight for Dixie. That cost him promotion. His patriotic reputation was redeemed only when, nine months later, he was shot to death leading the charge at Franklin. The prospect of the Confederate government's buying or renting male slaves as soldiers to be freed after victory brought on a weird frenzy of slave-selling. But, in the last weeks of its existence, the Confederate congress threw aside its scruples and passed the Negro Soldier Law authorizing enrollment of 300,000 slaves with a legal loophole to freedom if the South won the war.

Too late. There now were more black men under arms in blue than there were soldiers on the fighting lines in all the gray armies.[147] Seventy-five percent of those black men in Federal uniforms were Southerners. These were the soldiers whom Lincoln said tipped the scales for Union victory. They

206 | Confederate Origins of Union Victory

would not be outweighed by black men in gray. With those black Union men under arms, a great cultural change swept into a reuniting United States – a change still in progress – and the Civil War, though it would drag on through more days of blood, was over.

Why Did the Confederate War Go Wrong?

The Confederate war inflicted immense damage on the American people. It killed at least 620,000 American soldiers fighting in the gray and blue armies and maimed and wounded many more.[148] The war caused the deaths – by disease, starvation, wounds, and overwork – of a probable several hundred thousand black slaves in the South. It killed an uncalculated number of civilians white, free black, and Native American/Indian in the South, North, and West. U.S. Census records show the war cut by nearly one-third the natural increase in the U.S. population in the years just after the Civil War, making the U.S. poorer by about three million live births.[149]

THE CONFEDERATE WAR WENT WRONG because major elements of Southern culture at the mid-point of the nineteenth century would not let it go right. The Civil War was about swift-changing social attitudes in the United States and Southern resistance to some aspects of those changes. The most fundamental shift was a new perspective on how Americans must treat each other and a growing understanding in the North, and among some people in the South, that slavery must be abolished. However, Southern white society supported by black slavery had resisted for many years all efforts to ameliorate or end slavery and now felt compelled to go to war against the United States to preserve slavery in an independent Confederate States of America. The South lost its war because its military and political leaders could not transcend the limits of the slave-based culture that helped bring on the Civil War.

Those limitations made it too difficult for the Confederacy to beat off a new form of management of military power directed by Ulysses S. Grant and supported by a rapidly industrializing and modernizing North. The clever taking advantage of Union battlefield blunders in the war's early years and the hell-raising power of Confederate soldiers could not be sustained in the face of the North's methodical grinding away of the Southern manpower and resources needed to continue the war. Not when the culture of the South denied the Confederacy the tools most needed to make up for those losses:

> *Black soldiers.* The Southern slave system with its concept that slavers had financial rights in other human beings as property and the racism that grew out of slavery prevented the Confederacy from replenishing its depleted armies with soldiers drawn from

a million black male slaves. White Southerners feared arming black men as slave-soldiers would fire vengeful slave revolt. Conscripting black men with a promise of freedom after victory undercut the purpose of a war to preserve slavery. This option was out.

World war for cotton. Insularity and disinterest in the workings of the greater world outside itself denied the South a full understanding of what Europe would and would not do for the Confederacy. Southern leaders failed to internationalize their war for two reasons: First, by claiming the evident rightness of their independence struggle made a moral claim on European armies while failing to accept the moral impact in Europe of the Emancipation Proclamation. And, second, by trying to blackmail Europe with a cotton embargo while ignoring the natural flexibility of capitalism in finding ways to compensate for the loss to European industry of Southern cotton. This option could not be made to work.

Strategic inflexibility. The attitude of a need to resist any and every change to a slave-based economy and society translated into an inflexible administration of the Confederate war. The South denied itself the ability to evolve its military strategy and to choose combat commanders and political leaders capable of fresh thinking. Staying the course with a mismanaged offensive-defense over four years while hoping for a battlefield spectacle to remake the war is not a war-winning program. When the North, after many failed strategies and commanders, found Grant with his five blue arrows, and used the Emancipation Proclamation to politically support him, the South had no fresh response. This option undercut all other options.

Choosing the wrong hero. A mid-century Southern popular culture of prideful hot-bloodedness and un-calculated violent action, driven in part by fear of slave revolt and resistance to outside pressure to join a modernizing course, combined with politically inflexible Confederate leaders to provide no better choice than John Bell Hood as the South's last hope to win the war in 1864. This option was no option at all.

Hood and his campaign show that any nation that denies itself the full use of all its resources because of a culture imbued with racism, an inability to understand the larger world and its honest place in the world, an obstinate adherence to a war plan when the enemy makes multiple strategic shifts, and an insistence on a cultural litmus test rather than war-winning skills in choosing military leaders is likely to lose its war.

The Confederate failure shows that, before a nation goes to war, it needs to understand why it thinks as it does and how that thinking can limit its perspective on the enemy and on its own choice of leaders and strategies to beat that enemy. Or the nation will go to war unprepared to achieve victory.

When the time comes that you and I as citizens must help our country decide to go to war, devise a war-fighting strategy, and chose war leaders, we need to remember how the South came to choose John Bell Hood and his Middle Tennessee campaign for the Confederate war's last decisive action. We need to ask ourselves, *Could we as Americans do that to ourselves again?* We need to ask ourselves, *Why?*

Afterword

Steven Hardesty is a military historian, combat veteran, and former U.S. diplomat. He was an assessor of strategic plans for U.S. Special Operations Command and devised and ran tabletop war games for the U.S. Marine Corps. He is a graduate of the United States Air Force Air War College. He has degrees from the Universities of California and Alabama. He served as an Army artillery officer in the Vietnam War and for thirty years as a diplomat for the U.S. Department of State. He is a partner in Black Swan Advisors, LLC, a national security consultancy in Alexandria, Virginia, U.S.A. He writes novels about the Vietnam War, including *Ghost Soldiers, War Lover, Saigon Blues,* and *Poisoned Hearts.* He blogs at stevenhardesty.com.

This book had its earliest origins in a chance meeting with Napoleonic scholar David G. Chandler at Great Missenden Abbey, England, in 1988. His lively analysis of strategic problems in the U.S. Civil War sparked in me a love for historical research.

Special thanks to Anthony D. Mc Ivor, editor of *Rethinking the Principles of War,* for his critique of an earlier draft of this manuscript.

Bibliography & Notes

Primary Sources

"The Lost Opportunity at Spring Hill, Tenn. – General Cheatham's Reply to General Hood." *Southern Historical Society Papers* 9 (1881), 540-1.

Alexander, Edward Porter. *Fighting for the Confederacy: The Personal Recollections of General Edward Porter Alexander.* Edited by Gary W. Gallagher. Chapel Hill NC: University of North Carolina Press, 1989.

Alexander, Edward Porter. *Military Memoirs of a Confederate: A Critical Narrative.* New York: Da Capo Press, 1993 reprint of 1907 edition.

Basler, Roy P., ed. *The Collected Works of Abraham Lincoln.* New Brunswick NJ: Rutgers University Press, 1953.

Bradford, Ned, ed. *Battles and Leaders of the Civil War.* New York: The Fairfax Press, 1988.

Chesnut, Mary. *A Diary from Dixie.* Edited by Isabella D. Martin and Myrta Lockett Avary. New York: Gramercy Books, 1997 reprint of 1905 or 1906 edition.

Commager, Henry Steele, ed. *Documents of American History.* New York: Appleton-Century-Crofts, Inc., 1949, fifth edition.

Commager, Henry Steele, ed. *The Blue and The Gray: The Story of the Civil Was as Told by Participants.* New York: The Fairfax Press, 1982.

Davis, Jefferson. *The Rise and Fall of the Confederate Government*. Gloucester MA: Peter Smith, 1871.

Davis, Varina. *Jefferson Davis: Ex-President of the Confederate States of America: A Memoir by His Wife*. Baltimore MD: The Nautical & Aviation Publishing Company of America, 1990 reprint of 1890 edition.

Freeman, Douglas Southall, ed. *Lee's Dispatches: Unpublished Letters of General Robert E. Lee, C.S.A. to Jefferson Davis and the War Department of the Confederate States of America, 1862-65*. New York: Putnam, 1957.

Grant, Ulysses S. *Personal Memoirs of Ulysses S. Grant*. New York: Bonanza Books, reprint of 1885 edition.

Hood J. B. *Advance and Retreat: Personal Experiences in the United States and Confederate States Armies*. New Orleans: G. T. Beauregard, 1880.

Howe, M. A. DeWolfe, ed. *Home Letters of General Sherman*. New York: Charles Scribner's Sons, 1909.

Johnson, Robert Underwood and Clarence Clough Buel, eds. *Battles and Leaders of the Civil War*. New York: The Century Company, 1888.

Johnston, Joseph E. *Narrative of Military Operations Directed During the Late War Between the States*. Bloomington IN: Indiana University Press, 1959.

Jones, J. B. *A Rebel War Clerk's Diary at the Confederate States Capitol*. Edited by Earl Schenck Miers. New York: Old Hickory Bookshop, 1935.

Kean, Robert Garlick. *Inside the Confederate Government*. Edited by Edward Younger. New York: Oxford University Press, 1957.

Longstreet, James. *From Manassas to Appomattox.* New York: Da Capo Press, 1992 reprint of 1896 edition.

Otis, Ephraim A. "The Nashville Campaign." In *Military Essays and Recollections,* edited by William Eliot Furness, Roswell H. Mason, and Mason Bross, 3:267-88. Chicago: The Dial Press, 1899.

Roman, Alfred. *The Military Operations of General Beauregard in the War Between the States: 1861-1865* (New York: Da Capo Press, 1994 reprint of 1884 edition).

Schofield, John M. *Forty-Six Years in the Army.* New York: The Century Co., 1897.

Sherman, William T. *Memoirs of Gen. W. T. Sherman.* New York: Charles L. Webster and Co., 1891.

Simpson, Brooks D. and Jean V. Berlin, eds., *Sherman's Civil War: Selected Correspondence of William T. Sherman, 1860-1865.* Chapel Hill NC: University of North Carolina Press, 1999.

Simpson, Brooks D., Stephen W. Sears, and Aaron Sheehan-Dean, eds. *The Civil War: The First Year Told by Those Who Lived It.* New York: The Library of America, 2011.

Strode, Hudson, ed. *Jefferson Davis, Private Letters.* New York: Harcourt, Brace & World, Inc., 1966.

Taylor, Richard. *Destruction and Reconstruction: Personal Experiences of the Late War.* New York: D. Appleton and Company, 1879.

The War of the Rebellion: A Compilation of the Official Records of the Union and Confederate Armies. Washington, D.C.: Government Printing Office, 1881-1901.

Watkins, Sam. *"Company Aytch" or, A Side Show of the Big Show and Other Sketches.* Edited by M. Thomas Inge. New York: Plume, 1999.

Welch, Spencer Glasgow. *A Confederate Surgeon's Letters to His Wife.* Marietta GA: The Continental Book Company, 1954.

Secondary Sources

"American War and Military Operations Casualties: Lists and Statistics," Congressional Research Service, January 2, 2015.

Ash, Stephen V. *When the Yankees Came: Conflict and Chaos in the Occupied South, 1861-1865.* Chapel Hill NC: University of North Carolina Press, 1995.

Ballard, Michael B. *A Long Shadow: Jefferson Davis and the Final Days of the Confederacy.* Jackson MS: University Press of Mississippi, 1986.

Beals, Carleton. *War Within a War: The Confederacy Against Itself.* New York: Chilton Books, 1965.

Belcher, Dennis W. *General David S. Stanley: A Civil War Biography.* Jefferson NC: McFarland & Company, Inc., 2014.

Catton, Bruce. *The Army of the Potomac.* Garden City NY: Doubleday & Company, Inc., 1962.

Cozzens, Peter. *This Terrible Sound: The Battle of Chicka-mauga.* Chicago: University of Illinois Press, 1992.

Creveld, Martin van. *Supplying War: Logistics form Wallen-stein to Patton.* New York: Cambridge University Press, 1978.

Cutting, Elisabeth. *Jefferson Davis, Political Soldier.* New York: Dodd, Mead & Company, 1930.

DeConde, Alexander. *A History of American Foreign Policy.* New York: Charles Scribner's Sons, 1971, second edition.

Donald, David, ed. *Why the North Won the Civil War.* New York: Collier Books, 1960.

DuBois, W. E. B. *The Gift of Black Folk: The Negroes in the Making of America.* Boston: The Stratford Co., 1924).

Dyer, John P. *The Gallant Hood.* New York: Konecky & Konecky, 1950.

Fischer, David Hackett. *Albion's Seed: Four British Folkways in America.* New York: Oxford University Press, 1989.

Flood, Charles Bracelen. *Lee: The Last Years.* Boston: Houghton Mifflin Company, 1981.

Foote, Shelby. *The Civil War: A Narrative.* New York: Random House, 1974.

Gallagher, Gary W. *The Confederate War: How Popular Will, Nationalism, and Military Strategy Could Not Stave Off Defeat.* Cambridge MA: Harvard University Press, 1997.

Gallagher, Gary. *Lee: The Soldier.* Lincoln NB: University of Nebraska Press, 1996.

Gugliotta, Guy, "New Estimate Raises Civil War Death Toll," *The New York Times*, April 2, 2012 <http://www.nytimes.com/2012/04/03/science/civil-war-toll-up-by-20-percent-in-new-estimate.html>

Hattaway, Herman and Archer Jones. *How the North Won: A Military History of the Civil War.* Chicago: University of Illinois Press, 1991.

Hensel, Howard M. *The Sword of the Union: Federal Objectives and Strategies During the American Civil War.* Washington D.C.: U.S. Government Printing Office, 1989.

Johnson, Paul. *The Birth of the Modern: World Society 1815-1830.* New York: HarperCollins, 1991.

Jones, Archer. *Civil War Command and Strategy: The Process of Victory and Defeat.* New York: The Free Press, 1992.

Jones, David R. "U.S. Air Force Combat Psychiatry." Brooks Air Force Base TX: USAF School of Aerospace Medicine, 1986.

Lewis, Lloyd. *Grant Takes Command.* Boston: Little, Brown Company, 1969.

Livermore, Thomas L. *Numbers and Losses in the Civil War in America: 1861-65.* Millwood New York: Kraus Reprint Co., 1977.

Lowry, Don. *Dark and Cruel War.* New York: Hippocrene Books, 1993.

Maurice, Frederick. *Statesmen and Soldiers of the Civil War: A Study of the Conduct of War.* Boston: Little, Brown, and Company, 1926.

McMurray, Richard M. *Atlanta 1864: Last Chance for the Confederacy.* Lincoln NE: University of Nebraska Press, 2000.

McMurry, Richard M. *John Bell Hood and the War for Southern Independence.* Lexington KY: University Press of Kentucky, 1982.

McPherson, James M. *Battle Cry of Freedom.* New York: Ballantine Books, 1988.

McPherson, James M. *War on the Waters: The Union and Confederate Navies, 1861-1865.* Chapel Hill NC: University of North Carolina Press, 2012.

McWhiney, Grady and Perry D. Jamieson. *Attack and Die: Civil War Military Tactics and the Southern Heritage.* University AL: University of Alabama Press, 1982.

Miller, Brian Craig. *John Bell Hood and the Fight for Civil War Memory.* Knoxville TN: University of Tennessee Press, 2010.

Millet, Allan R. and Peter Maslowski. *For the Common Defense: A Military History of the United States of America.* New York: The Free Press, 1984.

Murray, Williamson, MacGregor Knox and Alvin Bernstein. *The Making of Strategy: Rulers, States, and War.* New York: Cambridge University Press, 1994.

O'Connor, Richard. *Hood, Cavalier General.* New York: Prentice-Hall, Inc., 1949.

Patrick, Rembert W. *Jefferson Davis and His Cabinet.* Baton Rouge: Louisiana State University Press, 1944.

Pratt, Fletcher. *Eleven Generals: Studies in American Command.* New York: William Sloane Associates, 1949.

Ross, Ishbel. *First Lady of the South: The Life of Mrs. Jefferson Davis.* New York: Harper & Brothers Publishers, 1958.

Russell, Thaddeus. *A Renegade History of the United States.* New York: Free Press, 2010.

Scaife, William R. *Hood's Campaign for Tennessee.* Atlanta: William R. Scaife, 1980.

Shiman, Philip. "Conspiring to Command? Speculations for the Motives of John Bell Hood in 1864." Paper presented at the annual meeting of the Society for Military History, Washington, DC, April 7-10, 1994.

Steele, Matthew Forney. *American Campaigns.* Washington D.C.: United States Infantry Association, 1922.

Sword, Wiley. *Southern Invincibility: A History of the Confederate Heart.* New York: St. Martin's Press, 1999.

Sword, Wiley. "The Other Stonewall." Civil War Times (February 1998): 36-44.

Symonds, Craig L. *A Battlefield Atlas of the Civil War.* Annapolis MD: The Nautical and Aviation Publishing Company of America, 1983.

Warren, Robert Penn. *Jefferson Davis Gets His Citizenship Back.* Lexington KY: The University Press of Kentucky, 1980.

Wiencek, Henry. *An Imperfect God: George Washington, His Slaves, and the Creation of America.* New York: Farrar, Straus and Giroux, 2003.

Wilson, Edmund. *Patriotic Gore: Studies in the Literature of the American Civil War.* New York: Oxford University Press, 1966.

Wood, W. J. *Civil War Generalship: The Art of Command.* Westport CN: Praeger, 1997.

Woodworth, Steven E. *This Great Struggle: America's Civil War.* New York: Rowman & Littlefield Publishers, Inc., 2011.

Woodworth, Steven E. *Jefferson Davis and His Generals.* Lawrence KS: University Press of Kansas, 1990.

Notes

[1] "They [European powers] hoped for our ruin!" said Cassius Clay, U.S. Consul in St. Petersburg, Russia: "They are jealous of our power. They care neither for the South nor the North. They hate both." Quoted in David Donald, ed., *Why the North Won the Civil War* (New York: Collier Books, 1960), 57.

[2] Quoted in Carleton Beals, *War Within a War: The Confederacy Against Itself.* (New York: Chilton Books, 1965), 7.

[3] The Thirteenth Amendment to the U.S. Constitution meant to make slavery permanent was finally passed by Congress and ratified by the states in December 1865 *abolishing* slavery in the United States.

[4] The United States slave system that resulted is movingly described in historian Henry Wiencek's *An Imperfect God: George Washington, His Slaves, and the Creation of America* (New York: Farrar, Straus and Giroux, 2003). A curious supplement to Wiencek's analysis are the anecdotes describing white master envy of black slaves' unique emotional and intellectual "freedoms" under the slave system in Thaddeus Russell's *A Renegade History of the United States* (New York: Free Press, 2010).

[5] If black slaves are included in the count, as they should because the Confederacy eventually tried to bring them into its armies, Southern illiteracy was seven or eight times higher than in the North.

[6] Quoted in David Hackett Fischer, *Albion's Seed: Four British Folkways in America* (New York: Oxford University Press, 1989), 260.

[7] Frederick Douglass, "The Late Election," *Douglass' Monthly*, December 1860, in Brooks D. Simpson, et al. (eds.), *The Civil War: The First Year Told by Those Who Lived It* (New York: The Library of America, 2011), 60.

[8] "Dixie" was a black character in an antebellum stage play and Dixie's Land meant the country of the slave. When Confederate forces marched, they sang slave ballads such as "The Yellow Rose

of Texas," wore "butternut" slave cloth, and fired bullets made by slaves.

⁹ *Richmond Enquirer*, June 1862, in Gary Gallagher, *Lee: The Soldier* (Lincoln NB: University of Nebraska Press, 1996), 283. Diary entry for June 12, 1861, J. B. Jones, *A Rebel War Clerk's Diary at the Confederate States Capitol* (New York: Old Hickory Bookshop, 1935), 1:51.

¹⁰ On February 15, 1865. Jones, *A Rebel War Clerk's Diary*, 2:422.

¹¹ Richard Taylor, *Destruction and Reconstruction: Personal Experiences of the Late War* (New York: D. Appleton and Company, 1879), 60.

¹² *The War of the Rebellion: A Compilation of the Official Records of the Union and Confederate Armies* (Washington, D.C.: Government Printing Office, 1894), Ser. 1, 28, 2:173, hereafter cited as *OR*.

¹³ Southern newspapers were government-controlled or self-censored and, until Federal troops tramped past a Southern farmhouse, the occupants rarely had any factual idea how badly their war was going. So far as they knew, contrary to the death lists and their own hungry bellies, happy gray armies were advancing on every front and the mongrel blue troops were retreating in ragged disorder because that is what their newspapers told them. Ulysses S. Grant, *Personal Memoirs of Ulysses S. Grant* (New York: Bonanza Books, reprint of 1885 edition), 2:251

¹⁴ Quoted in Bruce Catton, *The Army of the Potomac: Glory Road* (Garden City NY: Doubleday & Company, Inc., 1962), 240.

¹⁵ For contrast, the overall casualty rate in the Vietnam War was less than eight percent and in World War II less than six percent. Gary Gallagher, *The Confederate War: How Popular Will, Nationalism, and Military Strategy Could Not Stave Off Defeat* (Cambridge MA: Harvard University Press, 1997), 28-30.

¹⁶ New York City considered seceding into neutrality in order to remain the center of the South's cotton trade: "With our aggrieved brethren of the Slave States, we have friendly relations

and a common sympathy." "Mayor Fernando Wood's Recommendation for the Secession of New York City," January 6, 1861, in Henry Steele Commager, ed., *Documents of American History* (New York: Appleton-Century-Crofts, Inc., 1949, fifth edition), 1:374-76.

[17] Paul Johnson, *The Birth of the Modern: World Society 1815-1830* (New York: HarperCollins, 1991), 308.

[18] Edmund Wilson, *Patriotic Gore: Studies in the Literature of the American Civil War* (New York: Oxford University Press, 1966), 62. Alexander DeConde, *A History of American Foreign Policy* (New York: Charles Scribner's Sons, 1971, second edition), 247.

[19] An engagement between the *USS Wyoming* and Japanese sea and land forces, July 16, 1863, in the Shimonoseki Strait, near Yokohama, Japan.

[20] Quoted in Wiley Sword, *Southern Invincibility: A History of the Confederate Heart* (New York: St. Martin's Press, 1999) 59.

[21] John M. Schofield, *Forty-Six Years in the Army* (New York: The Century Co., 1897), 190.

[22] Quoted in Edward Porter Alexander, *Military Memoirs of a Confederate: A Critical Narrative* (New York: Da Capo Press, 1993), 302. The quotation may be apocryphal. Longstreet does not mention the comment in his own memoir and Alexander cites the sentence as "it is told that."

[23] The story of the $500,000 Burnside owed Preston is told in Mary Chesnut, *A Diary from Dixie*, edited by Isabella D. Martin and Myrta Lockett Avary (New York: Gramercy Books, 1997 reprint of 1906 edition), 159. Chesnut's book is a post-war memoir in diary form.

[24] Peter Cozzens, *This Terrible Sound: The Battle of Chickamauga* (Chicago: University of Illinois Press, 1992), 111.

[25] *OR* Ser. 1, 42, 2:1259.

[26] James Longstreet, *From Manassas to Appomattox* (New York: Da Capo Press, 1992 reprint of 1896 edition), 386-87.

²⁷ Richard O'Connor, *Hood, Cavalier General* (New York: Prentice-Hall, Inc., 1949), 174. A view disputed by historian Philip Shiman in "Conspiring to Command? Speculations on the Motives of John Bell Hood in 1864" (paper presented at the annual meeting of the Society for Military History, Washington, DC, April 7-10, 1994).

²⁸ J. B. Hood, *Advance and Retreat: Personal Experiences in the United States and Confederate States Armies* (New Orleans: G. T. Beauregard, 1880), 62.

²⁹ The survival rate for leg amputation in the Confederate armies was forty-one percent. Brian Craig Miller, *John Bell Hood and the Fight for Civil War Memory* (Knoxville TN: University of Tennessee Press, 2010), 90.

³⁰ Winfield Scott first had suggested rolling battle to squeeze the life out of the Confederacy. From the beginning of the war, Lincoln had tried to foist that concept on his unwilling generals. So had Henry Halleck in his 1862 shift of Federal strategic vision from capturing territory to destroying enemy armies. Army commander William S. Rosecrans had pushed the idea in early 1863. See Grant's war plan and April 4, 1864, orders to Sherman to "get into the interior of the enemy's country as far as you can, inflicting all the damage you can against their war resources." *OR* Ser. 1, 32, 3:246.

³¹ Grant, *Personal Memoirs*, 1:49-50.

³² Across the four years of war, a million bales got through the U.S. Navy's blockade and into Europe or went overland into Mexico. Another million were traded across the combat frontier into the Northern black market to preserve starving Southern families or to feed Confederate armies. Lee's soldiers ate New York bacon paid for in black market cotton. Two-and-one-half million bales rotted in Southern ports or were fired by retreating Confederates or enemy action or were used in cotton-clad fighting

ships. Donald, *Why the North Won*, 95-97. Beals, *War Within a War*, 14. "During the war, the Confederacy managed to export between half a million and a million bales of cotton through the blockade...[but] almost 10 million bales [were] exported in the last three antebellum years." James M. McPherson, *War on the Waters: The Union and Confederate Navies, 1861-1865* (Chapel Hill NC: University of North Carolina Press, 2012), p. 225.

[33] Quoted in Shelby Foote, *The Civil War: A Narrative* (New York: Random House, 1974), 3:468.

[34] Brooks D. Simpson and Jean V. Berlin, eds., *Sherman's Civil War: Selected Correspondence of William T. Sherman, 1860-1865* (Chapel Hill NC: University of North Carolina Press, 1999), 609.

[35] Bruce Catton, *The Army of the Potomac: Stillness at Appomattox*, 37. With his appointment on March 9, 1864, as lieutenant general and general-in-chief of all Federal armies, Grant assumed an immense command – 662,000 men – and a new goad of ambition. That fabulous number is deceptive: subtract cooks, clerks, mule drivers, bandsmen and all the other support elements and he had 533,000 in combat arms. Subtract 40,000 infantry and cavalry fighting Indians or garrisoned in places far from combat and Grant had 490,000 effectives in the war theaters. Subtract a third pounding sentry duty by railroads and warehouses and he had 327,000 usable combat soldiers. That was about 60 percent more than the Confederacy could muster to its firing lines, a goodly increment but no guarantee of victory on the offensive against an enemy operating in friendly territory. Lloyd Lewis, *Grant Takes Command* (Boston: Little, Brown Company, 1969), 141.

[36] "By early 1864 almost half of Union troops in the field were occupying captured territory and guarding communications and logistical lines." Williamson Murray et al., *The Making of Strategy: Rulers, States, and War* (New York: Cambridge University Press, 1994), 236.

[37] Confederate desertions exceeded 100,000. Herman Hattaway and Archer Jones, *How the North Won: A Military History of the Civil War* (Chicago: University of Illinois Press, 1991), 444. Jones, *Rebel War Clerk's Diary*, 2:439. Charles Bracelen Flood, *Lee: The Last Years* (Boston: Houghton Mifflin Company, 1981), 20. Those deserters who crossed the lines were lost to the Confederacy permanently – the North re-uniformed them and sent them into the vast and anonymous West to fight Indians so that they would not be captured and hanged as traitors to the gray cause. Catton, *Army of the Potomac: Stillness*, 331. Over 200,000 Federal soldiers deserted during the war, a process that accelerated as the war progressed. 75,000 were arrested in the last two years. Henry Steele Commager, ed., *The Blue and The Gray* (New York: The Fairfax Press, 1982), 482.

[38] Sherman letter to his brother Senator John Sherman, July 29, 1864, in M. A. DeWolfe Howe, *Home Letters of General Sherman* (New York: Charles Scribner's Sons, 1909), 304.

[39] Lee and Johnston also had this bond: Lee's father was "Light Horse" Harry Lee, a cavalry commander for George Washington. Joe Johnston's father had been a major in Lee's Legion.

[40] Hood, *Advance and Retreat*, 144, 157.

[41] Matthew Forney Steele, *American Campaigns* (Washington D.C.: United States Infantry Association, 1922), 536. Sherman complained that Hood merely had to wait for Union furloughs to reduce Sherman's army by half in late summer in order for Hood to win at Atlanta, *OR* Ser. 1, 38, 5:609. Halleck to Grant, September 19, 1864: "...we are now not receiving one-half as many [men] as we are discharging. Volunteering has virtually ceased, and I do not anticipate much from the President's new call...Unless our Government and people will come square up to the adoption of an efficient and thorough draft, we cannot supply the waste of our army." *OR* Ser. 1, 37, 2:385.

[42] Quoted in Hattaway and Jones, *How the North Won*, 149.

---

[43] Howard M. Hensel, *The Sword of the Union: Federal Objectives and Strategies During the American Civil War* (Washington D.C.: U.S. Government Printing Office, 1989), 200. Varina Davis, wife of the Confederate president, calculated that Grant had in aggregate – initial force plus augmentees and replacements across the entire campaign – 192,000 troops against Lee's aggregate of 78,000. Varina Davis, *Jefferson Davis: Ex-President of the Confederate States of America: A Memoir by His Wife* (Baltimore MD: The Nautical & Aviation Publishing Company of America, 1990 reprint of 1890 edition), 2:492.

[44] Livermore reports the total Confederates engaged as 75,054 of which 3,903 were killed and 18,735 were wounded – 23,638 casualties. Thomas L. Livermore, *Numbers and Losses in the Civil War in America: 1861-65* (Millwood NY: Kraus Reprint Co., 1977), 103. James M. McPherson, *Battle Cry of Freedom* (New York: Ballantine Books, 1988), 732, and Hensel, *Sword*, 200, count 18,000. Gallagher, Gary, *The Confederate War*, 135, reports Lee's casualties at 30,000.

[45] Quoted in Frederick Maurice, *Statesmen and Soldiers of the Civil War: A Study of the Conduct of War* (Boston: Little, Brown, and Company, 1926), 108.

[46] Lee to Davis, June 26, 1864, *OR* Ser. 1, 37, 1:767.

[47] Sherman to Grant, April 10, 1864, *OR* Ser. 1, 32, 3:313.

[48] Lee to Davis, February 3, 1864. *OR* Ser. 1, 32, 2:667.

[49] *OR* Ser. 1, 38, 3:619. Johnston believed he was winning a campaign of attrition against Sherman, killing and wounding four Federal soldiers for every Confederate casualty. Richard M. McMurray, *Atlanta 1864: Last Chance for the Confederacy* (Lincoln NE: University of Nebraska Press, 2000), 96-7.

[50] Johnston's return for April 1864 shows 52,992 troops. With the addition of Leonidas Polk's corps, 71,235. Sherman's armies totaled 98,797. With the addition of James B. McPherson's forces, 123,262. The two armies were equal in artillery. Estimates by Federal General O. O. Howard in Ned Bradford, ed., *Battles and Leaders of the Civil War* (New York: The Fairfax Press, 1988), 493.

Estimates by Sherman in Commager, *The Blue and The Gray*, 931.
Hood estimated Johnston could have added another 5,000 by
"lessening the extra duty men" and putting them – clerks,
teamsters, musicians – on the fighting line. Hood, *Advance and
Retreat*, 87. Braxton Bragg quoted in Hood, *Advance and Retreat*, 90-
91, estimated that Johnston had at his call 91,000 effectives of
infantry, cavalry and artillery plus 15,000 extra duty men one-half
of whom could be sent to the battle line without impairing the
army's efficiency.

[51] Alexander McClurg quoted in Commager, *The Blue and the
Gray*, 1114. Martin van Creveld, *Supplying War: Logistics form
Wallenstein to Patton* (New York: Cambridge University Press, 1978),
112.

[52] O. O. Howard's remark in Bradford, *Battles and Leaders*, 495.

[53] Grant, *Personal Memoirs*, 2:344-5, 2:167.

[54] Georgia's Governor Brown, "reasoning that one State had as
much right to disagree with eleven as eleven with twenty," offered
a radical states rights concept that could destroy any liberated
Confederacy. Taylor, *Destruction and Reconstruction*, 234.

[55] In a letter dated February 10, 1879, former Secretary of War
James Seddon wrote Davis that Lee was consulted after "the
determination had been made to relieve General Johnston" and
that the consultation "was designed merely to secure General Lee's
estimate of qualifications in the selection of a successor for the
command." Quoted in Jefferson Davis, *The Rise and Fall of the
Confederate Government* (Gloucester MA: Peter Smith, 1871), 2:561.

[56] Davis to Lee, July 12, 1864. On July 13, Davis wrote to Lee, "It
is a sad alternative, but the case seems hopeless in present hands."
OR Ser. 1, 52, 2:692.

[57] Douglas Southall Freeman, ed., *Lee's Dispatches: Unpublished
Letters of General Robert E. Lee, C.S.A. to Jefferson Davis and the War
Department of the Confederate States of America, 1862-65* (New York:

Putnam, 1957), 282-84. Lieutenant General William J. Hardee repeatedly refused the offer of command of the Army of Tennessee though he acted interim commander for some weeks between Bragg and Johnston. He later complained to a friend in petulant language that the president was "endeavoring to create the impression that in declining the command" in December 1863 he had "declined it for all future time." Davis, *Jefferson Davis*, 2: 451. "[F]eeling my inability to serve the country successfully" as army commander, he wrote Davis, "I respectfully decline the command if designed to be permanent." Hardee to Adjutant General Samuel Cooper, December 30, 1863, from Dalton, Georgia. OR Ser. 1, 31, 3:764-5. Cooper asked Hardee to recommend an alternative as commander, saying, "It is needless to name Lee, who is indispensable where he is." OR Ser. 1, 31, 3:775.

[58] OR Ser. 1, 38, 5:880.

[59] OR Ser. 1, 38, 5:881. Years later, Johnston wrote "I intended to defend Atlanta" but he said that to no one at the time. Joseph E. Johnston, *Narrative of Military Operations Directed During the Late War Between the States* (Bloomington IN: Indiana University Press, 1959), 363.

[60] OR Ser. 1, 39, 2:714.

[61] Hood was made full general on July 18, 1864, when he assumed command of the Army of Tennessee. His permanent rank remained lieutenant general.

[62] Richmond *Whig* of July 19, 1864, quoted in John P. Dyer, *The Gallant Hood* (New York: Konecky and Konecky, 1950), 251.

[63] Hood to Davis and Davis's reply, July 18, 1864, OR Ser. 1, 38, 5:888. Hood, *Advance and Retreat*, 142-3.

[64] The strangest and most amusing example was Davis's announcement that he "did not care to hear" any criticism against the North's greatest failed general, George B. McClellan, whom Davis proclaimed a military star. Longstreet, *From Manassas*, 66.

[65] Schofield, *Forty-Six Years*, 232.

[66] William T. Sherman, *Memoirs of Gen. W. T. Sherman* (New

York: Charles L. Webster and Co., 1891), 2:72.

[67] Sherman, *Memoirs*, 565. Livermore, *Numbers and Losses*, 122-6.

[68] Hood, *Advance and Retreat*, 202.

[69] *OR* Ser. 1, 38, 3:695.

[70] Hood to Bragg, September 4, 1864, *OR* Ser. 1, 38, 5:1018.

[71] Craig L. Symonds, *A Battlefield Atlas of the Civil War* (Annapolis MD: The Nautical and Aviation Publishing Company of America, 1983), 93. McPherson, *Battle Cry*, 750, 755. Symonds's and McPherson's dead and wounded casualty figures seem a good mean of estimates here. Estimates are all that can be expected of Civil War combatant and casualty figures: Federal forces kept relatively good records, Confederate forces did not, and the two sides did not measure the same things – the Union numbered all of its troops, the Confederacy counted "effectives"; the Union counted total arms, the Confederacy often, but not always, just combat arms and sometimes just the troops on the firing line, excluding officers, artillery, cavalry, stragglers, and non-combatants. Livermore gives an excellent discussion in *Numbers and Losses*, 66-70. Hood had the second worst casualty record of all Confederate generals, after the incompetent John C. Pemberton: His units averaged 19.2 percent in losses while inflicting just 5.5 percent on their enemies, a radical reversal of the usual ratio in which the resource-rich and "profligate" Union expended more lives for success than did the Confederacy. Grady McWhiney and Perry D. Jamieson, *Attack and Die: Civil War Military Tactics and the Southern Heritage* (University AL: University of Alabama Press, 1982), 22.

[72] McWhiney and Jamieson, *Attack and Die*, 19-22.

[73] Elisabeth Cutting, *Jefferson Davis, Political Soldier* (New York: Dodd, Mead & Company, 1930), 231-2. Hood, *Advance and Retreat*, 254.

[74] Hood, *Advance and Retreat*, 253.

[75] Roy P. Basler, ed., *The Collected Works of Abraham Lincoln* (New Brunswick NJ: Rutgers University Press, 1953), 8:27. Grant, *Personal Memoirs*, 345. Robert Garlick Kean, *Inside the Confederate Government*, edited by Edward Younger (New York: Oxford University Press, 1957), 176.

[76] Gary W. Gallagher, ed., *Fighting for the Confederacy: The Personal Recollections of General Edward Porter Alexander* (Chapel Hill NC: University of North Carolina Press, 1989), 496.

[77] Davis letter to a nephew, January 8, 1865. Hudson Strode, *Jefferson Davis, Private Letters* (New York: Harcourt, Brace & World, Inc., 1966), 139. Johnston had done himself no good in refusing to lay out his battle plans for his president – Rembert W. Patrick, *Jefferson Davis and His Cabinet* (Baton Rouge: Louisiana State University Press, 1944), 138 – whom he expected to tell all to the newspapers, but Hood did give Davis his plan, and Davis did hand it over to the newspapers.

[78] *OR* Ser. 4, 3:792.

[79] Archer Jones in *Civil War Command and Strategy: The Process of Victory and Defeat* (New York: The Free Press, 1992), 237. A Confederate senator from Mississippi wrote Davis on October 2, 1864, "Our State literally swarms with deserters..." *OR* Ser. 4, 3:707.

[80] *OR* Ser. 1, 44, 919, 932-3. Hood, *Advance and Retreat*, 280-1. Governor Brown to Davis, July 10, 1864: "If you will order 5,000 more muskets to Atlanta, I will try to furnish the number of old man and boys of the State to use them for the emergency. Please answer immediately." *OR* Ser. 1, 52, 2:691.

[81] John B. Hood, "The Defense of Atlanta," in *Battles and Leaders of the Civil War*, eds. Robert Underwood Johnson and Clarence Clough Buel (New York: The Century Company, 1888), 4:344.

[82] Hood, *Advance and Retreat*, 266-8.

[83] Contemporary sources vary widely on how many soldiers Hood commanded in his Middle Tennessee campaign – from 25,000 to 60,000. Hood said that he had 31,000 combat arms troops and that he was joined on the march by Nathan Bedford

Forrest's 5,000 cavalry. This figure appears to exclude – as was customary with Confederate counts – officers, artillerymen, and support personnel or "extra duty men." Hood, *Advance and Retreat*, 298. Sherman estimated that Hood commanded 35,000 infantry and 10,000 cavalry. Sherman to Halleck, January 1, 1865, OR Ser. 1, 39, 1:584. George Thomas thought Hood had 50-67,000 combat arms troops. Schofield, *Forty-Six Years*, 191. When Hood assumed command at Atlanta, the Army of Tennessee had 48,750 "effectives" – combat arms troops ready for action – including 1,500 Georgia militiamen. Steele, *American Campaigns*, 543. After casualty losses in the battles for Atlanta, Hood in his after action report (February 15, 1865) claimed to have a total of 43,500 effectives. Hood, *Advance and Retreat*, 325. This figure tallies with *OR*, Ser. 1, 38, 3:683. Considering post-Atlanta recruitment, additional soldiers sent to Hood in Alabama, the arrival of Forrest's cavalry, and losses to illness and desertion, 50,000 troops of all kinds is a reasonable estimate of the number Hood took into Tennessee. In support of Hood's campaign, Beauregard also sought to organize military activities elsewhere to draw Federal power away from Hood. For instance, in a December 2, 1864, letter to Edmund Kirby Smith, Beauregard wrote, "...Sherman's army has lately abandoned Atlanta on a venturesome march across Georgia to the Atlantic coast about Savannah. His object is, besides the destruction of public and private property, probably to re-enforce Grant to compel Lee to abandon Richmond. It is hoped that Sherman may be prevented from effecting his object, but should it be otherwise, the success of Hood in Tennessee and Kentucky would counterbalance the moral effect of the loss of Richmond. Hence the urgent necessity of either re-enforcing Hood or making a diversion in Missouri in his favor." OR Ser. 1, 45, 2:640.

[84] Quoted in General William B. Bate letter to Cheatham in "The Lost Opportunity at Spring Hill, Tenn. – General Cheatham's Reply to General Hood," *Southern Historical Society Papers* 9 (1881), 541.

85Quoted in Dennis W. Belcher, *General David S. Stanley: A Civil War Biography* (Jefferson NC: McFarland & Company, Inc., 2014), 207.

86 Hood, *Advance and Retreat*, 286-87.

87 Historian Steven E. Woodworth considers that "Hood convinced himself that he had not failed. His generals...had let him down...They were incompetent and probably cowardly, too. The soldiers, cowardly and afraid to charge an entrenched enemy, had also failed him." Steven E. Woodworth, *Jefferson Davis and His Generals* (Lawrence KS: University Press of Kansas, 1990), 299. Historians O'Connor and Don Lowry say that Hood so "raged" at his generals and "against the lack of spirit and ability among officers and men alike" that it "almost came to pistols at dawn, there and then." O'Connor, *Hood*, 234. Don Lowry, *Dark and Cruel War*, (New York: Hippocrene Books, 1993), 553. There is no eyewitness report to the story of the threat of a duel and neither historian cites a contemporary source.

88 Hood, *Advance and Retreat*, 297.

89 Hood, *Advance and Retreat*, 292.

90 OR Ser. 1, 45, 1:688.

91 Hood, *Advance and Retreat*, 296.

92 Wiley Sword, "The Other Stonewall," *Civil War Times* (February 1998), 42.

93 Allan R. Millet and Peter Maslowski, *For the Common Defense: A Military History of the United States of America* (New York: The Free Press, 1984), 225. Symonds, *A Battlefield Atlas*, 95. These are the most frequently cited casualty figures; they concur with Livermore.

[94] General Field Orders, No. 38, December 1, 1864. *OR* Ser. 1, 45, 2:628. Hood sent Seddon and Beauregard his first formal notice of his claimed victory at Franklin on December 3, 1864. The telegram was not received in Richmond until December 14, probably due to winter ice cutting Confederate telegraph lines and Federal cavalry raiding other means of communication. Hood followed this with a second brief and cryptic report on December 5. *OR* Ser. 1, 45, 2:643-4, 650. On December 7, 1864, Hood sent Beauregard a one sentence request – "Whenever you can I will be pleased if you could visit this army." – with no explanation offered. *OR* Ser. 1, 45, 2:659.

[95] Schofield, *Forty-Six Years*, 188.

[96] Livermore, *Numbers and Losses*, 131-2. Hood, *Advance and Retreat*, 298. John M. Schofield, *Forty-Six Years*, 258-9.

[97] Hattaway and Jones, *How the North Won*, 724.

[98] David R. Jones, "U.S. Air Force Combat Psychiatry" (Brooks Air Force Base TX: USAF School of Aerospace Medicine, 1986), 9.

[99] Jones, "U.S. Air Force Combat Psychiatry," 27.

[100] Hattaway and Jones, *How the North Won*, 410.

[101] Jones, "U.S. Air Force Combat Psychiatry," 14.

[102] Quoted in William R. Scaife, *Hood's Campaign for Tennessee* (Atlanta GA: William R. Scaife, 1980), 75.

[103] [103] Quoted in Fletcher Pratt, *Eleven Generals: Studies in American Command* (New York: William Sloane Associates, 1949), 200.

[104] Schofield estimated that, discounting troops ill or not equipped, Thomas had 30,000 in his entire department, 24,000 with Schofield, and 5,000 cavalry. Schofield, *Forty-Six Years*, 192.

[105] *OR* Ser. 1, 45, 2:685.

[106] Thomas to Halleck, December 12, 1864. *OR* Ser. I, 45, 2:155.

[107] Hood to Seddon, December 3, 1864, *OR* Ser. 1, 45, 3: 643-4.

[108] Grant to Thomas, *OR* Ser. 1, 45, 2:70, 2:97. Grant to Halleck, December 8, 1864, *OR* Ser. 1, 45, 2:96. Stanton to Grant, December 7, 1864, *OR* Ser. 1, 45, 2:84.

[109] Grant to Secretary of War Edwin M. Stanton, December 7,

1864. *OR* Ser. 1, 45, 2:84.

[110] Grant to Halleck, December 9, 1864, *OR* Ser. 1, 45, 2:115-6.

[111] That same day, December 13, a frustrated Grant ordered Major General Joshua A. Logan to Nashville to take the command instead of Schofield. *OR* Ser. 1, 45, 2:171.

[112] *OR* Ser. 1, 45, 2:180.

[113] For Schofield's version, see his *Forty-Six Years*, 237-9. Historian W. J. Wood reports the meeting occurred December 10 in the St. Cloud Hotel. Thomas told his generals about Grant's "preemptive order to attack" and the impossibility of doing so. The generals upheld Thomas. Thomas then gave his generals their orders for the battle, when conditions permitted action. Wood, *Civil War Generalship*, 214.

[114] *OR* Ser. 1, 45, 2:180.

[115] Grant got the news of the Nashville victory on December 15, 1864, while *en route* to Nashville. He stopped his journey and returned to the Army of the Potomac. *OR* Ser. 1, 45, 2:195.

[116] Livermore, *Numbers and Losses*, 132-33. Livermore reports total Federal forces engaged as 49,773 suffering 387 killed, 2,562 wounded and 112 missing in action; Confederate forces engaged as 23,207, killed and wounded unknown, 4,462 taken prisoner.

[117] Steven E. Woodworth, *This Great Struggle: America's Civil War* (New York: Rowman & Littlefield Publishers, Inc., 2011), 325.

[118] Quoted in Pratt, *Eleven Generals*, 211.

[119] Grant to Thomas, 11:30 PM, December 15, 1864. *OR* Ser. 1, 45, 2:195.

[120] Hood message to Beauregard and Seddon, December 17, 1864. *OR* Ser. 1, 45, 2:699. "Rumors...and the official reports of the enemy, seem to establish that General Hood has sustained a serious reverse." December 25, 1864. *OR* Ser. 1, 45, 2:733.

[121] Report of Surgeon George E. Cooper, U.S. Army, Medical Director, Department of the Cumberland, April 7, 1865, *OR* Ser. 1, 45, 1:111.

[122] Nathan Bedford Forrest to Richard Taylor, January 2, 1865: "The Army of Tennessee was badly defeated and is greatly demoralized, and to save it during the retreat from Nashville I was compelled almost to sacrifice my command." *OR* Ser. 1, 45, 2:756.

[123] Sam Watkins, *Company Aytch" or, A Side Show of the Big Show and Other Sketches*, edited by M. Thomas Inge (New York: Plume, 1999), 209.

[124] Ephraim A. Otis, "The Nashville Campaign," *Military Essays and Recollections* (Chicago: The Dial Press, 1899), 3:286.

[125] Kean, *Inside the Confederate Government*, 181.

[126] *OR* Ser. 1, 45, 2:757.

[127] Hood to Seddon, January 13, 1865. *OR* Ser. 1, 45, 2:781.

[128] Alfred Roman, *The Military Operations of General Beauregard in the War Between the States: 1861-1865* (New York: Da Capo Press, 1994 reprint of 1884 edition), 2:332. Seddon to Hood, January 15, 1865. *OR* Ser. 1, 45, 2:785.

[129] Hood asked to keep the command or to be given another, presumably of equal rank. Hood to Davis, January 16, 1865. *OR* Ser. 1, 45, 2:786.

[130] Roman, *Military Operations*, 2:333.

[131] Hood to Davis, January 23, 1865, *OR* Ser. 1, 45, 2:804. "I was ordered to Texas with instructions to gather together all the troops willing to follow me from that State, and move at once to the support of General Lee." Hood, *Advance and Retreat*, 311.

[132] C. J. McRae, Agent, Confederate States of America, to Seddon, July 4, 1864, describes the vessels. *OR* Ser. 4, 3:526, 529.

[133] Kean, *Inside the Confederate Government*, 192.

[134] Chesnut, *Diary*, 342.

[135] Hood's after action report for July 18-September 6, 1864, filed in Richmond on February 15, 1865, followed by Johnston's determination to prefer charges against Hood for statements made in the report. *OR* Ser. 1, 38, 3:628-38.

[136] McMurray, *John Bell Hood*, 183.

[137] Jones, *Rebel War Clerk's Diary*, 2:450.

[138] Chesnut, *Diary*, 373.

[139] Soldier's letter found in Raleigh, North Carolina, April 13, 1865, quoted in Spencer Glasgow Welch, *A Confederate Surgeon's Letters to His Wife* (Marietta GA: The Continental Book Company, 1954), 121.

[140] Foote, *The Civil War*, 3:756. About 200,000 Northern soldiers deserted during the war, but that was from a larger base number of troops.

[141] Stephen V. Ash, *When the Yankees Came: Conflict and Chaos in the Occupied South*, 1861-1865 (Chapel Hill NC: University of North Carolina Press, 1995), 240-41.

[142] Quoted in Ishbel Ross, *First Lady of the South: The Life of Mrs. Jefferson Davis* (New York: Harper & Brothers Publishers, 1958), 210. After Appomattox, in addition to the ruined Army of Tennessee, the Confederacy still had under arms 52,000 men in Florida and Georgia, 42,000 under Richard Taylor in Mississippi and Alabama, and 18,000 under Edmund Kirby Smith west of the Mississippi.

[143] Jones, *Rebel War Clerk*, 2:371, 388.

[144] Secretary of State Judah P. Benjamin speech at Richmond in February 1865, quoted in Michael B. Ballard, *A Long Shadow: Jefferson Davis and the Final Days of the Confederacy* (Jackson MS: University Press of Mississippi, 1986), 10.

[145] Quoted in Robert Penn Warren, *Jefferson Davis Gets His Citizenship Back* (Lexington KY: The University Press of Kentucky, 1980), 58.

[146] Catton, *Army of the Potomac: Stillness*, 226.

[147] 179,000 black soldiers and 10,000 black sailors in the Union army and navy. Across the entire war, Union armies employed an additional 200,000 to one million fulltime and occasional paid black laborers. W. E. B. Dubois, *The Gift of Black Folk: The Negroes in the Making of America* (Garden City Park NY: Square One Publishers, 2009), 83.

[148] 620,000 is the generally accepted figure for total Union and Confederate soldier deaths but newer calculations suggest the figure could be as high as 850,000. Guy Gugliotta, "New Estimate Raises Civil War Death Toll," *The New York Times*, April 2, 2012 <http://www.nytimes.com/2012/04/03/science/civil-war-toll-up-by-20-percent-in-new-estimate.html>. "American War and Military Operations Casualties: Lists and Statistics," Congressional Research Service, January 2, 2015, uses the traditional figure. Calculations by historians of civilian deaths directly attributable to the war range from 50,000 to 250,000.

[149] Calculation of U.S. Census Bureau data for all censuses from 1810 through 1900 shows an average increase of 31 percent per ten-year period for the U.S. white population (natural increase and immigration combined) and an average ten-year period increase of 23 percent for the U.S. black population (natural increase of slave and free blacks, assuming some additional slaves brought illegally into the U.S., slaves brought in with the admission of Texas as a state, and minimal, if any, foreign black immigration). The 1860 and 1870 censuses, however, show substantial decrease in the rate of population increase for both whites and blacks. Over the ten years including the Civil War and Reconstruction, the white population grew by twenty-five percent and the black population by ten percent. In other words, at the 1870 census, there were 1,600,000 fewer whites and 580,000 fewer blacks than could have been expected from the trend starting with the first census after the 1808 shutdown of the slave trade. However, the general trend of war-suppressed population growth is stark. Civil War deaths of soldiers and civilians, and the new births for which they may have accounted, as well as the post-war poverty of the South, explain the 1860-1870 retardation in U.S. population growth. The census statistics also show the effects of the Civil War fell more heavily on the black population than the white. Besides wartime overwork and hunger, slaves likely died from disease at the same rate as the soldiers spreading diseases

continent-wide – at the rate of two disease deaths for every combat death. It is interesting that Robert Garlick Kean, from his perspective in the Confederate War Department, noted in his diary an estimate that one million blacks had died during the war (Kean, *Inside the Confederate Government*, 213). A figure of that magnitude is not reflected in census statistics. However, if total civilian deaths directly attributable to the war were as high as 250,000, the death figure for slave and free black civilians caught up in the war zones could be one-third to one-half of the total civilian figure.

Made in the USA
Middletown, DE
24 January 2022

59528450R00149